**Production Board - Part I**

| D/E | Scene# | Set / Location | Pages | Cast (row values) |
|---|---|---|---|---|
| 1/8 E 32 | 32 | OFFICE BLDG. WINDOW | 1/8 | MAN PACKS EQUIP. (SE) |
| 1/8 E 13 | 13 | STREET/VAN TRUCK | 1/8 | GIRLS FIX MAKE-UP (C) |
| 1/8 E 30 | 30 | PANEL VAN TRUCK | 1/8 | LAUGHTER FROM WITHIN — 25 (C) |
| | | DAY 8 | | |
| D 12 I 12 | 12 | PANEL VAN TRUCK | 4/8 | 1,2,3,5 — SURVEILLANCE OF COUPLE 25 (SE) |
| D 14,16 I 14,16 | 14,16 | PANEL VAN TRUCK | 2 1/8 | 1,2,3 1/2o,3 1/2o,5 — DISCUSS SURVEILLANCE (C)(SE) |
| D 27 I 27 | 27 | PANEL VAN TRUCK | 1 3/8 | 2 1/2o,3 1/2o,5,6 — THEY PAY PAUL, LISTEN (SE)(C) |
| D 29 I 29 | 29 | PANEL VAN TRUCK | 5/8 | 5 — HARRY MAKES A JOKE (SE) |
| N 46 I 46 | 46 | AMY'S BLDG. HALL - APT. | 2/8 | 1 — 16 1/2,16 — CLIMBS STAIRS, ENTERS APT. (10) |
| N 47 I 47 | 47 | AMY'S APT. | 5/8 | 1 — HARRY VISITS AMY |
| | | **DAY 11 — WEEK TWO** | | |
| D 104 E 104 | 104 | AMY'S APT. BLDG. | 1/8 | 1 — ENTERS BLDG. (10) |
| D 105 I 105 | 105 | AMY'S BLDG. HALL | 2/8 | 2 1/2o. — OPENS AMY'S DOOR |
| D 106 I 106 | 106 | AMY'S APT. | 1 3/8 | 2 1/2o,3 1/2o. — AMY'S GONE |
| D 108 I 108 | 108 | AMY'S APT. | 1/8 | 1 — STANDS IN EMPTY APT. |
| | | **DAY 12** | | |
| D 98 I 98 | 98 | ELEVATOR - DIRECTORS | 6/8 | 1 — 29,30,31 — 25 RIDES CROWDED ELEVATOR |
| D 199 I 199 | 199 | ELEVATOR | 1/8 | 1,2 — RIDES ELEVATOR, HOLDING TAPES |
| D 276-291 I 276-291 | 276-291 | ELEVATOR | 7/8 | 1 — 10 ANN ENTERS ELEVATOR |
| D 366-368 I 366-368 | 366-368 | FINANCIAL PLAZA - MR.C'S | 5/8 | 1 — 50 SEES NEWS HEADLINE |
| | | **DAY 13** | | |
| D 200 I 200 | 200 | LOBBY | 1/8 | 1 — 1 EXITS ELEVATOR |
| D 201-205 I 201-205 | 201-205 | MAZE - CORRIDORS | 7/8 | 1 — M WALKS, MEETS DOG |
| D 273 I 273 | 273 | DIR'S. P.H. RECEPTION | 2/8 | 1 — 20,20,20,20 — 15 WALKS THROUGH RECEP. AREA |
| D 274 I 274 | 274 | DIR'S. P.H. CORRIDOR | 5/8 | 1 — 20,20 WALKS TO DIRECTOR'S DOOR |
| D 275 I 275 | 275 | DIRECTOR'S OFFICE | 2/8 | 1,2 — OFFICE IS EMPTY |
| D 369-376 I 369-376 | 369-376 | DIR'S. P.H. RECEPTION | | 3,7 — 75 THEY SEE EACH OTHER |
| | | **DAY 14** | | |
| D 99 I 99 | 99 | DIR'S P.H. RECEPTION | 1 4/8 | 1,7 — TRIES TO MAKE DELIVERY |
| D 100 I 100 | 100 | DIR'S. P.H. CORRIDORS | 1/8 | 1,7 — HARRY FOLLOWS MARTIN |
| D 102 I 102 | 102 | DIR'S. P.H. CORRIDORS | 4/8 | 2 1/2o,3 1/2o,7 — 10 SEES MARK |
| D 101 I 101 | 101 | MARTIN'S OFFICE | 1 1/8 | 1 — TOLD DIRECTOR IS AWAY |
| | | **DAY 15** | | |
| D 206-221 I 206-221 | 206-221 | DIRECTOR'S OFFICE | 7 3/8 | 1,2 1/2o,3 1/2o,4,7 — A MEETS WITH MR.C. |
| D 223-224 I 223-224 | 223-224 | DIRECTOR'S OFFICE | 4/8 | 1,2 1/2o,4,7 — A LEAVES OFFICE |
| D 225 I 225 | 225 | ELEVATOR | 3/8 | 1,7 — THEY SAY GOODBYE |
| | | **DAY 16 — WEEK THREE** | | |
| D 93-99 I 93-99 | 93-99 | LAWYER'S OFFICE | 2 3/8 | 1 — 19,19 — 39 REVEALED AS OWNER, SEES TONY |
| D 95 I 95 | 95 | LAWYER'S OFF. & STUDY | 2 7/8 | 1 — TONY CRIES, TELLS STORY (10) |
| D 40 I 40 | 40 | HARRY'S APT. BLDG. FOYER | 3/8 | 1 — A CHECKS MAIL, GREETS NEIGHBOR |
| D 41 I 41 | 41 | HARRY'S APARTMENT | 1 | 1 — 11 HARRY CALLS APT. MANAGER |
| | | **DAY 18** | | |
| N 42 I 42 | 42 | HARRY'S APT. - KITCHENETTE | 1 1/8 | 1 — 12,13,14,15 — DISTURBED BY TENANTS |
| N 43 I 43 | 43 | HARRY'S APT. BLDG. FLOOR-HALL | 3/8 | 1 — 12,13,14,15 — BOB TALKS TO HARRY |
| N 44 I 44 | 44 | HARRY'S APT. | 3 5/8 | 1 — 11,12,13,14,15 — A BIRTHDAY PARTY |
| | | **DAY 19** | | |
| D 49 E 49 | 49 | HARRY'S APT. BLDG. | 1/8 | 1 — HARRY EXITS BUILDING |
| N 48 I 48 | 48 | HARRY'S APT. | 3/8 | 1 — M HARRY PLAYS SAX |
| N 377 I 377 | 377 | HARRY'S APT. BLDG. | 4/8 | 1 — 12,12,14,14 — PASSES RON ON STAIRCASE |
| N 378-379 I 378-379 | 378-379 | HARRY'S APARTMENT | 3 | 1 — 3 1/2o. — 18 1/2 TRIES MR.C'S OFFICE, CONFRONTS NEIGHBORS |
| | | **DAY 20** | | |
| D 92 E 92 | 92 | TELEPHONE BOOTH | 1 1/8 | 1 — 18 1/2 — 41 20 HE CALLS DIRECTOR |

**Title:** THE CONVERSATION  
**Director:** FRANCIS COPPOLA  
**Producer:**  
**Asst. Director:**  
**Prod'n Mgr.:** CLARK PAYLOW

### Character / Artist list

| No. | Character | No. | Artist |
|---|---|---|---|
| 1 | HARRY CAUL | | |
| 2 | ANN | | |
| 3 | MARK | | |
| 4 | MR. C. | | |
| 5 | STANLEY | | |
| 6 | PAUL MEYERS | | |
| 7 | MARTIN | | |
| 8 | WILLIAM P. MORAN | | |
| 9 | MEREDITH | | |
| 10 | MILLARD | | |
| 11 | MRS. GOETNER | | |
| 12 | RON KELLER | | |
| 13 | MRS. CORSITTO | | |
| 14 | BOB | | |
| 15 | BOB'S WIFE | | |
| 16 | AMY | | |
| 17 | LURLEEN | | |
| 18 | MALE SEC'Y | 19 | TONY |
| 20 | MALE RECEPT. | 21 | MIME |
| 22 | YOUNG MAN | 23 | YOUNG WOMAN |
| 24 | SHOPPER #1 | 25 | SHOPPER #2 |
| 26 | SHOPPER #3 | 27 | LAUNDRY LADY |
| 28 | #27'S LITTLE BOY | 29 | WOMAN #1 - ELEV. |
| 30 | WOMAN #2 - ELEV. | 31 | MAN IN ELEVATOR |
| 32 | DEMO MAN | 33 | SPEAKER |
| 34 | MAN IN BOOTH | 35 | YOUNG DRIVER |
| 36 | MOTEL CLERK | 37 | BUS DRIVER #1 |
| 38 | BUS DRIVER #2 | 39 | MC NAUGHT |
| 40 | NNCR / P.A. SYST. | 41 | TEL. OPER. #1 |
| 42 | CHROME DOME V.O. | 43 | WOMAN IN R-RM |
| 44 | TEL. OPER. #2 | 45 | MAN #2 IN BOOTH |

MUSIC: (M)  CARS: (C)  SPECIAL EQUIPMENT (SE)  ANIMALS: (A)  EXTRAS: (#)

### Scene strips

| Day/Nite | Breakdown Page # | Ext/Int | Scene | Location | No. of Pages | Characters present | Notes |
|---|---|---|---|---|---|---|---|
| D | 195-196 | E | 195-196 | FINANCIAL DISTRICT | 3/8 | 1 | CROSSES INTERSECTION |
| D | 197 | I | 197 | PLAZA AREA | 1/8 | 1 | WALKS THROUGH PLAZA |
| D | 198 | I | 198 | ELEVATOR AREA | 1/8 | 1 | HARRY SIGNS IN |
| D | 226-229 | E | 226-229 | TELEPHONE BOOTH | 4/8 | 1 | WALKS TO PHONE |
| D | 188-194 | E | 188-194 | GOLDEN GATE PARK — DAY 1 | 2 3/8 | 1, 5 | STAY AWAY FROM ME (M)(25) |
| D | 34 | E | 34 | ELECTRIC BUS | 1/8 | 1? | BUS MOVES ALONG (C)(25) |
| D | 36-37 | E | 36-37 | HARRY'S NEIGHBORHOOD | 2/8 | 1 | CROSSES STREET, GOES TO MKT (C)(25) |
| D | 35 | I | 35 | ELECTRIC BUS | 2/8 | 1 | HE EXITS BUS (25)(250 BUS) |
| D | 38 | I | 38 | NEIGHBORHOOD MARKET | 1/8 | 1 | SHOPS FOR DINNER (25)(20) |
| D | 365 | E | 365 | STREET - BURNING CAR — DAY 2 | 1/8 | 4 | CAR WRECKED IN FLAMES (C) |
| N | 45 | E | 45 | ELECTRIC BUS | 1/8 | 1 | EXITS BUS, ENTERS BLDG. (C)(10) |
| D | 96 | E | 96 | FINANCIAL DISTRICT — DAY 3 | 1/8 | 1 | CROSSES STREET / DIRECTOR'S BLDG (C)(25) |
| D | 97 | E | 97 | FINANCIAL PLAZA | 1/8 | 1 | WALKS TO ELEVATOR 25 |
| D | 271-272 | E | 271-272 | FINANCIAL PLAZA | 2/8 | 1 | PLAZA BUSY 75 |
| D | 282-283 | E | 282-283 | DIRECTOR'S BLDG. | 3/8 | 2 | FOLLOWS ANN TO BUS 37, 38 (25) |
| D | 1-9 | E | 1-9 | UNION SQUARE — DAY 4 | 3/8 | 2, 3, 6, 21, 22, 23 | SURVEILLANCE (M)(SE)(C)(125) |
| I | 58 | E | 58 | UNION SQUARE | 5/8 | 2, 3 | [REPEAT OPENING - "SEE SCENE 9"] |
| I | 62 | E | 62 | UNION SQUARE | 3/8 | 2, 3 | [REPEAT OPENING] |
| D | 64 | E | 64 | UNION SQUARE | 4/8 | 21 | ["REPEAT OPENING - SCN "9"] |
| D | 66 | E | 66 | UNION SQUARE | 3/8 | 2, 3 | [REPEAT ORIGINAL OPENING] |
| D | 68 | E | 68 | UNION SQUARE | 7/8 | 2, 3 | THEY TALK (C) |
| D | 71 | E | 71 | UNION SQUARE | 4/8 | 2, 3 | [REPEAT OPENING - SCN 25] |
| D | 87 | E | 87 | UNION SQUARE | 4/8 | 2, 3 | ANN KISSES MARK GOODBYE (C) |
| I | 107 | E | 107 | UNION SQUARE — DAY 5 / DAY 6 | 1/8 | 2 | [REPLAY - SCN #8 TI] (25) |
| | | | | WEEK ONE | | | |
| D | 9-22 | E | 9-22 | UNION SQUARE | 1 1/8 | 2, 3, 6, 21, 24, 25, 26 | THEY ARE TAILED (504/125) |
| D | 81 | E | 81 | UNION SQUARE | 3/8 | 2, 3 | MARK'S VOICE DISTORTED "KILL US" |
| D | 28 | E | 28 | UNION SQUARE | 2/8 | 3 | COUPLE PARTS 125 |
| D | 33 | E | 33 | UNION SQUARE | 1/8 | 21 | MUSICIAN'S PACK UP (25) |
| D | 182 | E | 182 | UNION SQUARE | 1/8 | 21 | NO DIALOGUE 25 |
| D | 185 | E | 185 | UNION SQUARE | 1/8 | 21 | M.O.S. 25 |
| D | 222 | E | 222 | UNION SQUARE — DAY 7 | 3/8 | 2, 3, 6, 21 | [ANN & MARK WALK & DISCUSS PAUL] (25) |
| D | 10-11 | E | 10-11 | UNION SQUARE | 3/8 | 2, 3 | CLOSE-UP - ANN (SE) |
| D | 25-26 | E | 25-26 | EIFFEL TOWER/TOP | 5/8 | 2, 3 | SURVEILLANCE NEAR BONGOS (M)(SE)(125) |
| D | 17 | E | 17 | EIFFEL TOWER/TOP | 2/8 | 3½? | SURVEILLANCE FROM ROOF (SE) |
| D | 31 | E | 31 | EIFFEL TOWER/TOP | 1/8 | | MAN PUTS EQUIP. AWAY (SE) |
| D | 18 | E | 18 | UNION SQUARE | 2/8 | 2, 3 | THEY WALK & TALK (507/125)(SE) |
| D | 23-24 | E | 23-24 | OFFICE BLDG. WINDOW | 6/8 | 2, 3, 6, 21 | THEY DISCOVER PAUL (509/125) |
| D | 103 | E | 103 | UNION SQUARE | 4/8 | 2, 3 | [REPEAT OPENING - SCN #24] (25) |

**KEY:**  
Yellow = Day Exterior · Green = Night Exterior · White = Day Interior · Blue = Night Interior · Orange = Week Ending · Red = Holidays

**Francis Coppola's THE CONVERSATION**

Robin Rocket.

# Film Scheduling

Or, How Long Will It Take To Shoot Your Movie?

by

Ralph S. Singleton

The Complete Step-By-Step Guide To Professional
Motion Picture Scheduling

LONE EAGLE

FILM SCHEDULING
Or, How Long Will It Take to Shoot Your Movie?

*Copyright © 1984 by Ralph S. Singleton*

LONE EAGLE PUBLISHING CO.
9903 Santa Monica Blvd. Suite 204
Beverly Hills, CA 90212

*Printed in the United States of America.*

Cover painting and book design by Liz Vietor

FIRST EDITION, May, 1984

**Library of Congress Cataloging in Publication Data**

Singleton, Ralph S. (Ralph Stuart), 1940–
    FILM SCHEDULING, Or, How Long Will It Take To Shoot Your Movie?
    Includes index.
    1. Moving Pictures- -Production and direction- -Planning. I. Title.
II. Title: Film scheduling. III. Title: How long will it take to shoot your movie?
PN1995.9.P7S58   1984      791.43'0232      84–5691
IBSN 0–943728–11–8 (pbk.)

84 85 86 87 88

1 2 3 4 5 6 7 8 9 10

*Material from "The Conversation" reproduced with permission from Francis F. Coppola.*

iv

For
Francis Coppola

# TABLE OF CONTENTS

# ACKNOWLEDGEMENTS

I would like to thank those producers, production executives, production managers, first assistant directors and production accountants with whom I have worked and who have helped me over the years. Without their guidance, patience and friendship, this book would not have been possible. To name all those who have helped me over the years would fill another book, so I shall name just a few: Jacqueline Babbin, Jonathan Bernstein, Peter Cornberg, William Eustace, Paul Ganapoler, Wolfgang Glattes, David Golden, Sam Goldrich, George Goodman, Alex Hapsas, William Hassell, George Justin, Larry Kostroff, Charles McGuire, John Neukum, Charles Okun, Hal Polaire, Everett Rosenthal, Jonathan Sanger, Peter Scoppa, James Turner, Kenneth Utt, Herb Wallerstein and Ted Zachary.

A special thanks to Clark Paylow, the production manager of THE CONVERSATION.

One special individual guided this project from its formative period to its completion. Through her intelligence, perserverance and genuine belief in the idea, this book was born. There

is no one I can give more thanks than Joan Vietor, my editor
and publisher.

Ralph S. Singleton
Beverly Hills, California

# FOREWORD

When Ralph Singleton and I first met each other as DGA trainees in New York, we both wondered why there was no adequate text book on film production. We vowed that once we became production managers and figured out what was going on, we'd write that book ourselves. Well, as you can see, Ralph has done it. And not only one book, but four: this one on scheduling, one on budgeting, a workbook and a dictionary.

Laying out a schedule for a film (or television project) is a crucial first step towards launching your project successfully. No film can be budgeted properly without a schedule. A schedule can provide you with ways to talk intelligently about your screenplay and to base critical decisions (actors, locations, weather, etc.) on reality rather than the fantasy induced by the euphoria of making the deal.

Many people want to jump right from *the deal* to *the budget*. Unless that budget has been derived from a detailed analysis of the screenplay, it will be just another piece of fiction. Just as a good script is the foundation for a well-received film, a well-thought-out schedule is the foundation for an on-budget production.

The motion picture business is fascinating and complicated. During the years that I worked as a production manager/assistant director, countless numbers of people would ask me how I learned to prepare a budget and shooting schedule. I learned the way most production people do—on the job. It is only in the last few years that colleges and universities have begun offering specific courses on film production. But even with the advent of these courses, the amount of material written by working professionals has been sorely lacking. There are dozens of books on acting, directing, screenwriting and even producing, but not on the logistics of film production. *Film Scheduling* answers the questions of how to transform written words into a blueprint —the shooting schedule. Ralph has been a production manager/assistant director on feature films and television shows, both large and small. He has taken these years of experience and put them into readable, understandable terms. This is the best book on film scheduling that I have read.

*Film Scheduling* would have been a terrific help when I was starting out. I heartily recommend it to anyone who wants to learn about motion picture production—from students to studio executives, film buffs to financiers.


Jonathan Sanger

# AUTHOR'S NOTE

"*It's been done this way for sixty years, and'll probably be done this way for the next sixty.*" That's the answer I got when I'd ask around to see if there were any new production/budget forms that made a little more sense than the ones that I'd been using. Production managing a motion picture is difficult enough without having to decipher and sift through the multitude of forms and formats available on the market today. None of those forms really offered a logical progression or any sort of standardization from script breakdown to budget. After many years of vowing to do something about it, and many hours of discussion with other production veterans, I decided to do something about it and designed a whole set of production and budget forms. You'll see some of them here, and some in *Film Budgeting,* but most of them are in *The Film Scheduling/Film Budgeting Workbook.* In later chapters, you'll learn about COLOR-CODING, and I think you'll be pleased to see how logical it makes things. The same color that is assigned to a category used when breaking down a script also carries through to the BUDGET FORM. The information on the BREAKDOWN SHEET is listed in the same order that it is on the budget form—less chance to miss something. The breakdown sheets themselves are printed on different color papers which correspond to the production strips—again, hopefully to save you time and reduce errors when you are trying to get ready for a production.

With this book, *Film Scheduling,* and the companion books, I hope to take some of the mystery out of film production management and streamline the process. It's taken a long time for this book to reach you. I'd love to hear your comments—praise or criticism—when you've finished. I'm also looking forward to seeing your name on the screen when future production credits roll.

R. S. S.

**Note:** Words in **BOLD-FACE SMALL CAPS** are defined in the glossary.

# Film Scheduling

**Filmmaker's Library**

# I
# INTRODUCTION

## THE SIX STAGES OF PRODUCTION

1. Wild Enthusiasm
2. Total Confusion
3. Utter Despair
4. Search for the Guilty
5. Persecution of the Innocent
6. Promotion of the Incompetent

Anon.

There is an adage which says, "It only takes two things to make movies: time and money." But HOW MUCH TIME? and HOW MUCH MONEY? How to find the answers to the first question will be found in this book—how to find the answers to the second question in the companion volume, *Film Budgeting*.

Whether you are a **PRODUCER** or a **PRODUCTION MANAGER**, whether you are working on a studio picture or trying to get your own independent feature off the ground, your ability to succeed will depend on how well you can answer these two questions.

Scheduling a feature film is a three-part process:

1) breaking down the script,

2) preparing a production strip board, and

3) determining the final shooting schedule.

Perhaps two obvious questions should be answered now: 1) Why is it necessary to break down a script? and, 2) Isn't there an easier and more reliable method?

To answer the first question, it is necessary to break down a script in order to be able to budget it, and ultimately, finance it. Breaking down a script is the process of taking each and every element in the script, accounting for it and scheduling it in the most expedient and cost-effective manner. Once you have broken down a script and created the PRODUCTION STRIP BOARD and SHOOTING SCHEDULE, you will be able to move on to the next step: budgeting. Remember—if you cannot schedule a picture, you cannot budget it.

To answer the second question, yes, we feel that there is an easier and potentially more reliable method than the rather out-moded version of pick-up-sticks (the production strip board) which we still use today, and that method employs a computer. We say "potentially" because the human element is still the most important part of effective scheduling and budgeting a feature film. Micro-processors are being used in almost every other phase of motion picture making these days, and hopefully they will soon also be used by producers, production managers and AUDITORS. Although there are companies using computers for their SCRIPT BREAKDOWNS and production scheduling in addition to their budget preparation and daily accounting functions, the practice is not yet widespread enough to consider it the norm. Therefore, we have chosen to show you our version of the system which is currently in use.

Many of you have looked at a production strip board and wondered how in the world anyone could create something so complicated. Take heart. At first glance, analyzing how long and how much seems like an impossible task. It is complicated and it is time-consuming, but it is not impossible. Although time is of the essence, you are not in a race. The extra time you spend and the care you take in breaking down your script and preparing your strip board and budget will be worth it—well worth it. Problems which are overlooked or neglected in the early stages of pre-production have an uncanny tendency of showing up later on in the production . . . and they cost a lot more to handle when there is a cast and crew standing around waiting.

This book was designed to give you real-life filmmaking situations and then show you how we suggest you handle them. We are extremely fortunate in being able to use the entire screenplay of *Francis Ford Coppola's* Academy Award nominated film, THE CONVERSATION, and include it in its entirety in *The Film Scheduling Film/Budgeting Workbook.* Although there is no such thing as a *typical* screenplay, we feel that THE CONVERSATION involves some of the most difficult situations you as a production person might encounter. In its designed complexity, the script has characters developing from the very first page. Unfortunately, this is very rare. If in your work you try to compare most scripts with THE CONVERSATION they will fall way short of the mark. The more we analyzed this screenplay, the more apparent was the writer's genius. After spending over one year analyzing its construction in great detail in order to write this book, it was not difficult for us to understand why this screenplay was nominated for an Academy Award. A great film begins with a great screenplay. This screenplay remained fresh and alive for us, even after the twentieth reading.

When you begin to break down the script and prepare the strip board and later on learn how to prepare a budget in the book *Film Budgeting,* you will learn the steps to follow for a Union and Guild production. We will refer to the specific Union and Guild regulations and adhere to them. We want you to learn to be prepared for the most professional and most difficult situations. If you can prepare for the worst then chances are you might be pleasantly surprised in almost any other situation. For those of you wanting to adapt these techniques to 16mm and 8mm productions, the major changes will occur when it comes to budgeting—your scheduling techniques should remain the same.

We have designed this series of books to be used by everyone involved in or interested in being involved in motion picture production. There is no better method to learn how to schedule and budget a feature film than by actually doing it. *The Film Scheduling/Film Budgeting Workbook* contains the entire script of THE CONVERSATION, plus sample forms of everything you will need in scheduling and budgeting a feature film project. If you follow the steps outlined in *Film Scheduling* and *Film Budgeting* you will be able to produce your own production board and feature film budget.

In *Film Scheduling,* you will see the making of a movie through the eyes of a production manager. Almost every successful producer or director in Hollywood will tell you that, aside from him- or herself, there is perhaps no one person more important to the successful evolution of a motion picture's schedule than the production manager. He or she is responsible to the director, the producer, the CREW, the ACTORS, the FINANCIERS, the INSURANCE COMPANIES, the COMPLETION BOND COMPANIES, the STUDIO, etc.

A good production manager must be able to find out what makes everyone on the picture tick—from the EXECUTIVE PRODUCER to the GOFER—and find ways for everyone to work together harmoniously (hopefully). Frequently, the production manager is asked to break down the script and prepare the board and budget before the director is hired. The production manager must be able to read the script and make initial decisions from the director's point of view in terms of how a particular scene is going to be shot, how much equipment is going to be needed, etc.

Rarely does an INDEPENDENT PRODUCER have enough money beforehand to hire a production manager to break down the script and prepare a board and budget. Instead, what usually occurs is the producer takes a haphazard guess at what the final figures should be and then calls upon the production manager later on to "fix it." Or, as happens more frequently than not, deals are made by people not experienced in production (although highly qualified in their respective fields) and then the production manager is called upon to produce a "$5 million budget." Why $5 million? Because that's what the deal was made for!

By understanding how to prepare schedules, boards and budgets, the independent producer will not only save time and money by preparing a workable board and budget the first time out, but will also have a better working relationship with the person he chooses as production manager.

There are many different schools of thought on script breakdown and budget preparation—perhaps as many different methods as there are producers in Hollywood with scripts under their arms. What we are presenting here is our method. It works for us, and hopefully, it will work for you.

As we mentioned before, the best way to learn how to schedule and budget is to do it. For those of you who want to participate, the complete script of THE CONVERSATION and all the necessary production forms and sample budget forms are in *The Film Scheduling/Film Budgeting Workbook.* To assist you in understanding all the terminology that you will find in motion picture production, we created *The Filmmakers' Dictionary* of over 1,000 film terms.

We hope that you find these books which comprise *Filmmakers' Library* to be excellent references throughout your filmmaking career. GOOD LUCK and ENJOY!

# II

## BASIC RULES

Before we begin, here are three basic rules. They are common sense, but should never be forgotten.

Rule Number One: **IF IN DOUBT—ASK!**

Sounds simple enough. Any idiot would, right? Wrong. In pre-production, the only stupid question is the one you forgot to ask. Take for example, the surprised (and embarrassed) LOCATION MANAGER who forgot to ask whether the lights on the Lincoln Memorial and Washington Monument were on pre-set timers. While filming a feature directed by Sydney Pollack, the full company of over one hundred cast and crew were caught in a dilemma on a Friday night as the lights on the statues started to go out. With the quick assistance of the Washington, D.C. Parks Commission Police and the fast work of a GAFFER who was able to by-pass the switching boxes on the statues' lights, this little neglected question could have turned into a $100,000 disaster.

*But,* you say, *the mistake was the location manager's—not the production manager's.* Literally, you are right. However, on a production, the production manager is responsible for everything, and ultimately the blame will rest on his shoulders for not having asked the location manager if he checked about the lights. So, to help avoid future situations such as this, ASK QUESTIONS!!!

## Rule Number Two: **NEVER ASSUME ANYTHING**

If you *assume* anything on a motion picture project, you will most likely end up making an *ass* out of *u* and *me*. In the example listed in Rule Number One, the location manager *assumed* that the lights on the statues stayed on all the time, the production manager *assumed* that the location manager had taken care of checking about the lights, and the director *assumed* that everything was under control. Luckily, for the production it all worked out. It could have ended up being a really expensive mess.

## Rule Number Three: **ALWAYS C. Y. A.***

Make lists. Be organized. Check, double-check and triple check everything. By the time your project is ready to begin, you will know it better than anyone on the payroll. You will have analyzed it from every conceivable angle, and, ideally, come up with every imaginable thing that could go wrong and taken steps to prevent it from happening. In reality, all you will have done is reduce the number of problems which will occur.

As we said in the Chapter One, we are just as anxious as you are to enlist the aid of a computer in keeping track of all the details and are working to make that day come a little bit sooner. In the meantime, we are still going to have to do things by hand.

---

*Cover Your Ass.

# III

## THE SCRIPT

Those of you who have chosen to break down THE CONVER-SATION, please turn to *The Film Scheduling/Film Budgeting Workbook* and read the script. Those of you who have chosen to break down your own script, please now read it through entirely. **Do not attempt to break down a script without first reading it through at least once!**

This will be the first and only time that you will be able to read this script as a partial spectator, so enjoy it. Sit back and read the script as you would a good book. Don't rush it, but don't start to analyze it. Just become familiar with the story line, the characters' names, the locales, etc. Those of you using THE CONVERSATION might wish to remove the script from the book (the sheets are perforated), three-hole punch it and put it into a three ring binder. It will make it easier to work on when you begin breaking down the script.

As a production manager, you will receive scripts to break down that, literally, come in all shapes and sizes. Is there such as thing as a STANDARD SCRIPT FORMAT? Yes and No. Yes, there is a format which we prefer and is preferred by most of the producers and studios (and which you will see in Example

One which follows). No, for some reason, many, many scripts —especially those written and typed by newer and less experienced writers are typed in different formats. Examples of some of these are also included.

An average feature length film whose running time is between 90 and 100 minutes in length will have a screenplay of about 100 to 120 pages when typed in the format shown in Example One. All your future estimates of how long it will take to film a particular scene will be based on the length of that scene. As we will discuss in a later chapter, the smallest fraction of a screen page is one-eighth. You will start to get a feeling for how long it will take to shoot an eighth of a page. When the script is typed in a different format so that either more information or less information is included in that eighth of a page, it is is easy to see how this will affect your calculations. Here, then, are examples of the same page from THE CONVERSATION typed in different formats.

(see next page)

16    CONTINUED                                           16

> HARRY
> (smiling)
> Since when you supposed to be entertained?

> STANLEY
> Sometimes it's nice to know what they're talking about.

> HARRY
> (half to himself)
> I don't care what they're talking about. I just want a nice fat recording.
> (indicates the headset)
> How you doing?

> STANLEY
> We're getting better than 40 percent.

> HARRY
> How about the second position?

> STANLEY
> Not so good.

Stanley turns the dial up on the sound recorder, and for a moment the conversation is doubled up on itself.

CUT TO:

17    TOP OF THE CITY OF PARIS - DAY                17

THE VIEW PANS from the man under the Eiffel Tower sign, across the park, to another man operating out of an open window of an office building. He is operating a second microphone identical to the first one we saw. It becomes clear that the young couple are being tracked from two opposing positions. We HEAR the young man laughing.

18    VIEW ON THE COUPLE                         18

> MARK
> Where'd you hear that?

> ANN
> (also laughing)
> My secret.

CUT TO:

Analyzing this format from the top, you will see that we have noted *Continued* at the top of the page next to the scene number to indicate that the scene is continued from the previous page. The scene numbers are listed on both sides of the page at the beginning of the scene. There are no spaces between the names of the characters and their dialogue, but there is one space left between the name of the scene and the first line of description.

(*Continued*) is marked again at the bottom of the page to indicate that the scene continues to the next page, or *Cut To,* if the scene ends. If the dialogue continues to the next page, (*More*) should be typed directly under the dialogue. The page number is marked in the upper right hand corner. There are no periods after scene numbers to differentiate them from page numbers. For those of you who may have to type a script, we have included the proper margin settings. For now, just analyze the visible differences you see among the following examples.

## Margin Settings

| | | |
|---|---|---|
| 12 | - | Scene Numbers - Left Hand |
| 18 | - | CONTINUED, SCENE NAME, left-hand margin. |
| 30 | - | Begin dialogue |
| 38 | - | Dialogue directions (these can also be centered). |
| 44 | - | Character names and (MORE) |
| 61 | - | End of dialogue |
| 65 | - | (CONTINUED), CUT TO, FADE TO, DISSOLVE TO, etc. |
| 73 | - | Scene Numbers - Right Hand |
| 78 | - | Page Number |

                              HARRY
                         (smiling)
            Since  when  you  supposed  to  be
            entertained?


                              STANLEY
            Sometimes it's nice to know what
            they're talking about.


                              HARRY
                         (half to himself)
            I   don't   care   what   they're
            talking  about.   I  just  want  a
            nice fat recording.
                         (indicates the headset)
            How you doing?


                              STANLEY
            We're  getting  better  than  40
            percent.


                              HARRY
            How about the second position?


                              STANLEY
            Not so good.

                              HARRY
                        (smiling)
           Since when you supposed to be
           entertained?


                              STANLEY
           Sometimes it's nice to know what
           they're talking about.


                              HARRY
                        (half to himself)
           I don't care what they're
           talking about. I just want a
           nice fat recording.
                        (indicates the headset)
           How you doing?


                              STANLEY
           We're getting better than 40
           percent.


                              HARRY
           How about the second position?


                              STANLEY
           Not so good.


Stanley turns the dial up on the sound recorder, and
for a moment the conversation is doubled up on itself.

TOP OF THE CITY OF PARIS - DAY
THE VIEW PANS from the man under the Eiffel Tower sign,
across the park, to another man operating out of an
open window of an office building. He is operating a
second microphone identical to the first one we saw.
It becomes clear that the young couple are being
tracked from two opposing positions. We HEAR the young
man laughing.
VIEW ON THE COUPLE


                              MARK
           Where'd you hear that?


                              ANN
                        (also laughing)
           My secret.
19    VIEW ON THE MIME
      He laughs, as he does a burlesque of the two of them
      walking for an amused crowd.
20    MOVING VIEW OF MARK AND ANN
      Ignorant of the Mime, still walking


                              MARK
           How do you feel?


                              ANN
           Oh, you know.

14

Although the two extreme opposite examples in Examples Two and Three may seem to be gravely exaggerated, they are samples of actual formats used today. As you can see by comparing them with Example One—the preferred format—the page count that you will end up with will be seriously affected by the way the script is typed. Obviously an eighth of a page of a script typed in the format shown in Example Two is going to be a lot less material to cover than the eighth of a page in Example Three. The more scripts you break down, the more experience you will garner in gauging scene length and when to make allowances and adjustments. For now, just be aware of the differences.

## Color Sequences

When revisions are made to FINAL SCRIPTS it is necessary to differentiate between old pages and new pages. The following color-code system is standard in the industry.

1. White
2. Blue
3. Pink
4. Yellow
5. Green
6. Goldenrod

If the writer or person typing the revisions can put an asterisk (*) in the right-hand margin of the line in which there is a change, it will make your job easier. Dialogue changes won't affect your board, ordinarily, but everything else will and can. You won't have to waste time searching for the change if it has been marked.

# IV
## THE BREAKDOWN SHEET

Breaking down the script to prepare for the production board is a painstaking task. It is also one of the most important parts of scheduling a film. If you forget something during this step, it will surely come back to haunt you. So, as patronizing as this sounds, find yourself a comfortable, quiet, airy room which has good light and claim it! Make sure you will be able to leave your work undisturbed for the duration of the time you are preparing your breakdown and production strip board. Don't start marking any information on your breakdown sheets until you have completely read the following instructions and information.

Gather your materials together and have them within arm's reach. The materials you will need to begin are:

### Breakdown Tools
- colored breakdown sheets. (100 each
     of blue, white, green and yellow.)
- several #2 lead pencils
- a transparent ruler

- six water-based fine-tipped marking
      pens in red, orange, yellow,
      green blue, violet.
- a three-hole punch

**Note:** We recommend using WATER-BASED MARKING PENS as they do not bleed through the paper. For those of you who are going to break down THE CONVERSA-TION, we recommend that you use colored pencils or crayons. Most scripts are not printed on both sides of the paper, and even the best water-based markers have been known to bleed through slightly. You won't run into this problem when working on a script which is printed on only one side of the paper.

On your next reading of the script, you are going to go through scene by scene and mark every bit of information relative to a single scene on the appropriate breakdown sheet. Because motion pictures are usually shot OUT-OF SEQUENCE (meaning Scene 1 could be shot on the last day of the schedule and Scene 34 on the first day), and you will be grouping all the DAY SHOTS in the same location together and all the NIGHT SHOTS in the same location together, we have found that it is easier and simpler to *color code* the breakdown sheets. In this way, later on, you will be able to tell at a glance whether a scene is an Interior or an Exterior, a Day scene or a Night scene. Take a look at the sample BREAKDOWN SHEETS at the end of this chapter. Samples of colored breakdown sheets are in *The Film Scheduling Film Budgeting Workbook.* Later, when you start transferring information from the breakdown sheets to the PRODUCTION STRIPS for the PRODUCTION STRIP BOARD, you will see that we have used the same colors for the strips as we have for the breakdown sheets. Although it is a little more expensive to use color-coded sheets, we feel it is better and more reliable in the long run. When you have been hired to prepare a board and budget, you will be under the gun time-wise and will need all the help you can get. Physically having to re-read the breakdown sheets every time you want to know whether a scene is an Interior or not is a waste of valuable time.

The color-code for the breakdown sheets (and production strips) is as follows:

|  |  |  |
|---|---|---|
| YELLOW | - | Exterior Day |
| WHITE | - | Interior Day |
| GREEN | - | Exterior Night |
| BLUE | - | Interior Night |

Three-hole punch your sheets so they may be stored in a three-ring binder. Don't let your sheets flop around loose—they can get lost. As soon as you complete the information on one sheet, put it into the binder. You are going to be creating your all-important production board and shooting schedule from these sheets.

## The Breakdown Sheet

1. **Date:** Put in the date you prepare the breakdown sheets, e.g., March 22, 1984.

2. **Key:** Reminder of the color-codes for the sheets and strips. The small numbers appearing in the boxes refer to the accounting codes on the budget form. These are not of importance until you begin preparing a budget.

3. **Production Company:** The name of the production company goes here.

4. **Production Title/Number:** The name of the show, e.g., THE CONVERSATION, goes here. Production compa-

nies which have more than one project in production/ development usually assign production numbers. If known, put than number in here.

5.  **Scene No:**   The definition of a scene changes from person to person, but for the production manager, it is a unit of action which takes place in the same location over the same period of time. If either the location or the time period changes, then the scene ends and a new one begins. A corollary to this rule says that if the number of actors/ actresses in a scene changes dramatically either at the beginning or the end of a scene, then perhaps a new scene number should be introduced. Most scenes are easily recognizable because the writer has marked INT. (Interior) or EXT. (Exterior) next to the description of the scene **(Union Square - Day)**. However, many times there are scenes hiding within easily identifiable scenes which should be broken out and counted separately. An example of this is in the Warehouse Party scene when suddenly Harry and Meredith are left alone. Originally, Scenes 173 and 174 were all Scene 173. In analyzing the scene, it became obvious that we didn't need to have all the other actors in the Scene 173 available to work in what is now Scene 174 when we only needed Harry and Meredith. So, we split Scene 173 into two scenes and made the second Scene 174.

Sometimes the converse is true. Oftentimes if the writer of the project is also the director, he will break the scene down into shots. Turn to page one of THE CONVERSATION. Strictly speaking, there is only one scene on this page, **Ext. Union Square - Day.** But, either Mr. Coppola or Mr. Clark Paylow, (the production manager of THE CONVERSATION) broke this scene into shots. When this happens, do not combine shots back into scenes. Consider each shot as a separate scene and do a separate breakdown sheet for each. It is always better to be more detailed than less detailed when it comes to breaking down a script.

It is usually a production manager's responsibility to number the scenes. Save the numbering until you are ready to transfer the information onto breakdown sheets. You may find that on subsequent readings, there are scenes which should be separated. When numbering your scenes, always number your screenplay on both sides. It makes identification of the scenes much easier.

### Added and Omitted Scenes

Go back to the example of Scene 173 and Scene 174. If you had already numbered your script and then decided to divide Scene 173 into two scenes, instead of re-numbering (and then re-typing) the entire script, simply mark the new scene, *Scene 173A.* Don't forget to adjust the breakdown sheets and create a new one for the new scene. If you OMIT a scene, then mark, *Scene 189 - Omitted* on both sides of the screenplay.

6) **Scene Name:** For Scenes 1 through 8 on page 1 of THE CONVERSATION, the official SCENE NAME is **Union Square/Park.** After reading this script through, we know that the story takes place entirely in San Francisco, California, so there is no need to be any more detailed than **Union Square/Park.** If we were changing cities or moving to very specific locations within Union Square, then it would be necessary to be much more detailed, such as: **Union Square/Park, San Francisco,** or **Union Square/ Park - Northeast Corner.**

7) **Description:** This is a brief description of the main action in the scene. As you are going to have to transfer this information to a very small space on a strip, keep this description as brief, yet as concise as possible. For Scene 1, the description would be, *Street musicians play "Red Red Robin".*

8) **Breakdown Page Number:** This number should correspond to the scene number unless the script you are breaking down has been numbered previously and there are scenes which have been ADDED (usually noted by a letter following a scene number, e.g. "24A") or DELETED (usually noted, "Scene 23 - Omitted"). Unless you find that scenes numbers have been improperly marked, leave the pre-numbered scenes as is. Make sure that you note on a separate piece of paper the numbers of all added and deleted scenes so that you will be able to double-check later on.

9) **Int. or Ext.:** These are abbreviations for Interior and Exterior. Referring to page 1 of THE CONVERSATION, all the scenes on that page are Exteriors—they take place OUTSIDE. Always write out INT. or EXT., not "I" or "E" in the space provided on the Breakdown Sheets.

10) **Day or Night:** Self-explanatory. Again, make sure that you write out DAY or NIGHT in the space provided. If DAWN or DUSK is specifically mentioned or inferred, then write out DAWN or DUSK instead.

**Note:** Now that you have determined that Scene 1 is a Day/Exterior, you know that the color of your first breakdown sheet will be YELLOW.

11) **Page Count:** This is an area of controversy among production managers. Traditionally, pages of script have been
broken down into eighths of a page for easy calculation,
although there are some production managers who prefer
to use tenths. We prefer eighths. If your screenplay has
been typed in fairly standard format (see Chapter Three),
then there will be about eight or nine inches of typed copy
per page. An eighth of a page, then, equals approximately
one-inch of typed copy. Anything less than one-inch is
always marked, 1/8. Be on the lookout for extra-long
pages and extra-short pages. Just because the writer/typist
put more copy (or less copy) on a page does not mean that
you should always have eight eighths. Some of your pages
will only be 3/8 long. Others will be over 8/8 (e.g. 1-2/8,
etc.) Some scenes are only 1 line long—they are still
marked as 1/8.

When dividing your script into eighths, use your transparent ruler. It is approximately one-inch wide. Using a pencil, draw a line at the beginning of each scene and at the
end of each scene. Measure the area and determine the
length. A scene 2" long will be 2/8, 3" long - 3/8, etc. Do
not convert your fractions—leave them as eighths. It
makes it easier to add and subtract later on. For scenes
longer than 1 page, mark 1-3/8, not 11/8. Full pages
should be marked as "1", not 8/8. Same reason. Always
circle the number and write it in the right hand margin.

**Note:** Many of you will be tempted to begin your breakdown by lining the script all the way through and then
going through and breaking out the elements. **Do not do
this. Take each scene one at a time.** You may find that at
first glance what appears to be one scene actually is two
and you will have to re-calculate.

CODE — BREAKDOWN SHEETS/STRIPS
Day Ext. — Yellow
Night Ext. — Green
Day Int. — White
Night Int. — Blue
Numbers refer to
budget categories ②

# SCRIPT
# BREAKDOWN SHEET

① DATE

③ ④ ⑧

PRODUCTION COMPANY ⑤    PRODUCTION TITLE/NO. ⑥    BREAKDOWN PAGE NO. ⑨

SCENE NO. ⑦    SCENE NAME    INT. OR EXT. ⑩

DESCRIPTION    DAY OR NIGHT ⑪

PAGE COUNT

| CAST<br>Red (1301-2-3) ⑫ | STUNTS<br>Orange (1304) ⑬ | EXTRAS/ATMOSPHERE<br>Green (1322) ⑮ |
|---|---|---|
| | EXTRAS/SILENT BITS<br>Yellow (1321) ⑭ | |
| SPECIAL EFFECTS<br>Blue (2300) ⑯ | PROPS<br>Violet (2500) ⑰ | VEHICLES/ANIMALS<br>Pink (2600/4500) ⑱ |
| WARDROBE<br>Circle (3400) ⑲ | MAKE-UP/HAIR<br>Asterisk (3500) ⑳ | SOUND EFFECTS/MUSIC<br>Brown (5100,5300,5400) ㉑ |
| SPECIAL EQUIPMENT<br>Box ㉒ | PRODUCTION NOTES ㉓ | |

©1984 Lone Eagle Productions, Inc.

## Marking The Elements On The Script Page

We have completed the description part of the breakdown sheet and have now come to the individual elements: Numbers 12-23 (beginning with CAST). Using the water-based pens (or crayons/colored pencils), we will color-code these elements using a system which we feel makes it much easier and simpler. The best way to mark the elements is to UNDERLINE—not highlight. During the course of the production, this marked and lined script may have to be photocopied. If highlighter pens are used over the typewritten copy, chances are it will be difficult (or sometimes impossible) to read or photocopy. By underlining, not only will you be able to read the words, but you will also be able to use brighter, more easily identifiable colors than you would with highlighters. **Remember: Do not mark anything on your script until you have read this chapter completely** When you start going through each scene to find the elements, the extra step of marking that particular element in a certain color on the script is, in effect, a cross-checking safe-guard. You will 1) read the script, 2) color-code the element on the script, and 3) write down the element on the breakdown sheet. We suggest using a pencil on the breakdown sheets in case you find something you have to change or delete.

The color-coding system is as follows:

| Color | | Element |
|---|---|---|
| **RED** | - | **CAST - SPEAKING** |
| **ORANGE** | - | **STUNTS** |
| **YELLOW** | - | **EXTRAS - SILENT BITS** |
| **GREEN** | - | **EXTRAS - ATMOSPHERE** |

| BLUE | - | SPECIAL EFFECTS |
| VIOLET | - | PROPS |
| PINK | - | VEHICLES/ANIMALS |
| BROWN | - | SOUND EFFECTS |

Circle all the WARDROBE information, mark all MAKE-UP and HAIR information with an Asterisk, and put a box around all SPECIAL EQUIPMENT information. Any other pertinent information should be underlined in black and listed under Production Notes (using a pen, not a marker.)

Inside each box you will notice four things: 1) the name of the category, such as CAST, 2) the name of a color (*red*) in parentheses to remind you which color you should be using when highlighting this information, and 3) a number also in parentheses (*1301-2-3*). These numbers correspond to the budget form categories. They are not of importance to you now, but will be in the future when you transfer all this information to the budget form.

Before marking anything, please read through all this information.

12) **Cast - Speaking:** UNDERLINE IN RED any person who utters one single word in the script. They are considered to have a SPEAKING part and must be scheduled and paid according to Screen Actors Guild (SAG) rules. PRINCIPALS are the leads in the film (Harry Caul, Ann and Mark would be Principals). SUPPORTING PLAYERS are the actors who have large parts, but are not the leads. (Stanley, Paul, Martin, etc., are Supporting Players.) DAY PLAYERS are actors who have only a few lines or a few scenes. (e.g., the people who live in Harry's apartment building are Day Players. So are Tony, Harry's niece, and

McNaught, Harry's attorney.) This information will be important later on when you begin to lay out your schedule and also when you do your budget. But for now, you will list all SPEAKING PARTS together here in the same category.

When you begin marking your script, UNDERLINE the character's name (or any element which you are marking) the first time it appears on the page, and then again on every succeeding page. If it is not mentioned again on the next page, but it is implied, write it in the margin and mark it with the appropriate color highlighter.

The first time a speaking part is mentioned in a scene, mark the character's full name in capitals (e.g., *HARRY CAUL*) on the breakdown sheet. Every time thereafter, you can use his first and/or last name, but it should be written in lower case (e.g., *Harry* or *Harry Caul*) By doing this, you will be able to tell later on when all your breakdown sheets have been re-shuffled that you have not missed any of the characters, and in which scene an actor first appears in the script.

If the actor in your script is a child, note the age the child is to play and list a WELFARE WORKER/TEACHER under production notes.

13) **Stunts:** UNDERLINE IN ORANGE. Any hazardous, or potentially hazardous, act or action which will be performed by a specially-trained person instead of the main actor is a stunt. If you find when reading through your script that there seems to be a fair amount of stunt work, then you will probably need a STUNT COORDINATOR in addition to the STUNT DOUBLES. Mark STUNT COORDI-

NATOR under PRODUCTION NOTES for the corresponding scene and the name of the CHARACTER and STUNT DOUBLE under CAST MEMBER.

In Scene 365, we see Mr. C. in his wrecked Mercedes Benz slumped over the steering wheel. In the next second, the car bursts into flames. Depending on how close the director wants to get, we may either use a Stunt Double or a DUMMY which would be made by SPECIAL EFFECTS. Make sure that you mark both possibilities under Production Notes and *Mr. C.* and *Mr. C - Stunt Double* under *Cast - Speaking.* It may also be necessary for the actor playing Mr. C. to be there for CLOSE-UPS. In THE CONVERSATION, the actor (Robert Duvall) was required to be present.

14) **Extras - Silent Bits:** UNDERLINE IN YELLOW any actor who, under direction, performs an action or causes an action to be performed in a scene which then becomes part of the story line.

Referring to Scene 17, the MAN ON THE EIFFEL TOWER with the shotgun microphone who tracks Ann and Mark as they make their way through Union Square Park is a SILENT. Silents or SILENT BITS are EXTRAS who have been UP-GRADED to a higher pay scale, but not as high as DAY PLAYER.

Refer now to Scene 3 where the Young Mime is dressed as a Drum Major. We have a tricky problem here—is this character a Silent? or a Speaking Part? By nature, mimes are silent. You could carry this logic to an extreme and say that if you were to do a film with Marcel Marceau he would be a Silent. Common sense has to prevail, though and tell you that if Marceau were one of the leads in the film, he would be listed as a "Principal" and therefore "Speaking" part. In this scene, however, the Young Mime imitates a man carrying a cup of hot coffee. The "man" turns out to be Harry Caul. Because in this scene, the Mime interacts with the main character and, in fact, *talks* to the surrounding crowd, we have listed the Mime as a speaking part and underlined his character in red. An equally logical case can be built for listing the Mime as a Silent. When you get into budgeting, you'll see that the rate for a "Speaking" actor is much higher than for a "Silent." We prefer to err on the high side.

15) **Extras - Atmosphere:** UNDERLINE IN GREEN. Atmosphere actors (aka Extras) are the actors who fill in the background and make the film look real. In the opening scenes of THE CONVERSATION (Specifically Scenes 1 and 2) the band which sets up and then later plays is listed as "Silent." But the "crowds of shoppers . . . and office workers out for their lunch hour" are listed as "Atmospheres." In this space on the breakdown sheet, you are going to make a rough estimate of how many people you are going to need and of what type (*how many office workers? how many shoppers?*). Your ability to guess accurately will improve with experience.

*Screen Actors Guild vs. Screen Extras Guild*

On the West Coast, all EXTRAS—Silents and Atmospheres —are under the jurisdiction of the Screen Extras Guild (SEG). There are very specific categories of EXTRAS with corresponding pay scales. In New York and Chicago, these separate categories exist, but all actors (including "Extras") are under the jurisdiction of the Screen Actors Guild (SAG). It is best to consult your local Screen Actors Guild and Screen Extras Guild.

16) **Special Effects:** UNDERLINE IN BLUE. To most people, Special Effects means only what they saw in RAIDERS OF THE LOST ARK, STAR WARS and ET. Special Effects means, literally, any effect which is special and which must be created. A working kitchen sink may not be *special* to you, but in movie terminology it is called a PRACTICAL SINK and falls under the category of SPECIAL EFFECTS. All the elements—fire, air and water—in all their various forms (rain, mud, hurricanes, floods, fires, etc.) and their resulting damage (exploding buildings, mountains caving in, avalanches, etc.) are all SPECIAL EFFECTS.

In Scene 43, "Harry cooks two porkchops." If this scene were shot in an actual apartment with a kitchenette, chances are that the stove would work. If this scene were shot on a stage, however, then a practical stove would have to be set up—SPECIAL EFFECTS DEPARTMENT.

17) **Props:** UNDERLINE IN VIOLET. Any portable object which is used in a scene by one of the actors is considered to be a PROP ("property") and comes under the jurisdiction of the PROP DEPARTMENT. If the object is part of the decor of the set, then it is considered SET DRESSING. As a particular prop may have to be made (or bought) in duplicate or triplicate, it is very important to list every single prop on the appropriate breakdown sheet.

Deciding where a prop is necessary may sometimes take some reading between the lines on your part. Re-read scenes 188 through 221. We FADE IN on Golden Gate Park where Harry confronts Stanley, CUT TO Harry walking to the Financial Plaza and into the elevator, and finally up to meet Mr. C. and Martin. In Scene 188, the easel with a large number 7 should be listed as a Prop. In Scene 189, Harry is carrying a blue plastic pouch which should be listed on Breakdown Sheet No. 189. As we know from reading the script, that blue plastic pouch contains the tape recording which Harry made of Ann and Mark. The pouch is not mentioned again until Scene 199, page 94, when he is inside the elevator. Although it is not specifically mentioned, it is possible that the blue plastic pouch could be seen in every single scene from 189 through 199. Therefore, you will need to mark, *blue plastic pouch* on those corresponding breakdown sheets.

18) **Vehicles & Animals:** UNDERLINE IN PINK. VEHICLES used to refer only to PICTURE CARS. We have expanded the category to refer to all vehicles which will be necessary in the scene. PICTURE CARS are vehicles used by the PRINCIPAL ACTORS in a scene, or which play a major part in the action of the scene. ATMOSPHERE VEHICLES are all other vehicles which are seen on the screen.

Refer to Scene 143 where Harry and group are in the parking lot of the St. Francis Hotel. PAUL'S STAFF CAR is a PICTURE CAR. The rest of the parked cars in the lot as well as the "city traffic" which Paul pulls out into and joins are ATMOSPHERE CARS.

Note the number of PICTURE CARS and ATMOSPHERE VEHICLES which you will need in each scene. Again, you are going to have to use your imagination. If the director is going to shoot this from a HIGH, WIDE ANGLE where you will see a lot of cars in the parking lot and on the street, you will need more than if he stays in very CLOSE. This is a question which only your director can answer, so make a note of it. When you mark, "Paul's Staff Car" make sure you also describe it (a grey sedan with a code number on the side). Later on in Scene 155 you will notice in the screen directions that a "mobile telephone receiver" is mentioned. Make sure that you go back to Breakdown Sheet No. 143 (and wherever else Paul's Staff Car is mentioned) and make a note of it. Most likely, a special antenna will have to be added to the hood of the car. Also, remind yourself to check and see if there is a special license plate which a staff car should carry. Your ART DEPARTMENT will need to know this.

ANIMALS in a scene require special handling. For each animal, or group of animals (such as horses, cows, sheep, etc.) you are going to need a TRAINER/HANDLER or WRANGLER. If the animal is required to perform special tricks or actions, then a specially-trained animal and trainer will be required. Many times, as in the case of Benji (or Lassie), there was not just one particular dog, but rather a group of look-alike dogs—each of which had been taught to do a specific action or trick.

In Scenes 202, 204 and 205, a large, black, Doberman Pinscher—obviously a trained attack dog—appears at the corridor. Mark the description of the dog under Vehicles and Animals and Handler—Attack Dog under Production Notes. As the dog appears quite calm in this scene, it may not be necessary to have a full-fledged attack-trained dog. Maybe just a trained Doberman will suffice. Make a note and ask the director.

19) **Wardrobe:**  Put a **CIRCLE** around any piece of wardrobe information described in the script and list it here. Most often, the wardrobe worn by the principal players will have to be available in duplicate or triplicate. In

scenes where the wardrobe is intentionally ripped or soiled, it is not uncommon to have a dozen or more copies of wardrobe available for RE-TAKES

20) **Make-Up and Hair:** Mark all make-up and hair references with an ASTERISK and list here. These notations will be especially important if the project is a PERIOD PIECE as more time will have to be allowed to prepare the actors before going on the set.

21) **Sound Effects & Music:** UNDERLINE IN BROWN. Any sound which must be recorded or pre-recorded should be listed here. Birds chirping, applause, or, as you see in Scene 1, the song—*Red, Red, Robin.* When a song such as that is needed in a particular scene, make a note under Production Notes that you will have to obtain (and pay for) the rights to use this song.

THE CONVERSATION poses a particular problem with regard to Sound Effects as a large portion of the screenplay refers to pre-recorded dialogue. When we go through the schedule, you will see what we mean. For now, just note and be aware of scenes which will involve playback of an original recording.

22) **Special Equipment:** BOXED IN BLACK. Unless specifically noted in a scene, you will have to use your imagination and common sense to mark any necessary equipment in this category. Again, you will have a lot of questions to ask the Director. If the scene says, ZOOM IN then you will require a special ZOOM LENS. If the scene says, SLOW MOTION, then you will need a VARIABLE SPEED MOTOR which will allow you to film at a rate faster than the normal 24 frames per second. If it seems

that the shot is going to be taken from a helicopter, then you should note that you will need a special HELICOPTER WITH A CAMERA MOUNT and perhaps another CAMERA OPERATOR who has been trained in helicopter work.

Referring again to Scene 143 in the *Parking Lot - Hotel St. Francis,* you may find out that the director would like to shoot this from a high, wide angle, necessitating a CRANE. Or, perhaps the director would like to follow along with the car as it drives out of the Parking Lot. This could be accomplished by using either a DOLLY or a CAMERA MOUNT on a CAMERA CAR, the latter could follow the car into traffic and stay with it.

In THE CONVERSATION, you will see that special SURVEILLANCE EQUIPMENT is needed. Mark SURVEIL-LANCE EQUIPMENT under Props, and also under Special Equipment. As soon as we have more details, we will include them. Note that you will need a TECHNICAL AD-VISOR for all this surveillance equipment to ensure the accuracy in the film. Don't get lazy and mark it just once —mark SURVEILLANCE EQUIPMENT under Special Equipment and TECHNICAL ADVISOR under Production Notes (See 23) every time they are mentioned or inferred in the script.

23) **Production Notes:** UNDERLINED IN BLACK (pen—not marker.) Throughout this chapter, we have mentioned things which should be included under Pro-duction Notes: Wardrobe, Technical Advisors, Animal Handlers, Welfare Worker for Child Actors, etc. List all your questions about a particular scene in this area as well as anything which you need to clarify with the director.

You will create your **SHOOTING SCHEDULE** and your **PRO-DUCTION BOARD** from these **BREAKDOWN SHEETS**. Although not a great deal of information can fit onto a strip, the Shooting Schedule should and does contain all the pertinent facts. Be detailed and be accurate.

Before you begin your breakdown of THE CONVERSATION; read over the following scenes and the corresponding breakdown sheets which we have as examples.

Her big eyes follow at the spot where he stood for a
while, and then she lies back down on the bed.

                                                   CUT TO:

48        INT.  HARRY'S SMALL LIVING ROOM - NIGHT               48

The single room is dominated by a large homemade
loudspeaker, a single speaker as in the old Hi Fi days.
We HEAR a Jazz record, old, but well-preserved.

THE VIEW ALTERS and reveals Harry seated on a
straight-back wooden chair in the center of his Living
Room, holding a saxophone, and furiously playing along
with the recording.

The sax solo finishes, to great applause from the live
audience, and a sweating, winded Harry closes his eyes
and takes it for himself.

                                                   FADE OUT:

FADE IN:

49        EXT. HARRY'S BUILDING - DAY                           49

A construction crew has begun work on the demolition of
an abandoned row of Victorian buildings.  We HEAR
sounds of trucks and hammers.  Harry exits the
building, passes the construction work and sits and
waits at the stop for the electric bus.

                                                   CUT TO:

50        EXT.  WAREHOUSE AREA - DAY                            50

Harry walks parallel to some railroad tracks in the
industrial part of the city.  Trucks double park, and
there is loading and unloading in progress.  Perhaps a
train goes by.

Harry steps into the warehouse building, pushes a
button, and rises up into the building.

                                                   CUT TO:

51        INT.  HARRY'S WAREHOUSE OFFICE - DAY                  51

Harry rises in an industrial elevator up into the
warehouse area.  We notice benches with electronic
equipment, some cabinets and shelves, a screened-off
area.  Stanley is lounging around on an old sofa
reading a magazine.

                                          (CONTINUED)

                      PAGE 28

# The Breakdown Sheet

Day Ext. — Yellow
Night Ext. — Green
Day Int. — White
Night Int. — Blue
Numbers refer to
budget categories

## SCRIPT
## BREAKDOWN SHEET

DATE *MARCH 22, 1984*

*48*
BREAKDOWN PAGE NO.

| PRODUCTION COMPANY | PRODUCTION TITLE/NO. | |
|---|---|---|
| *48* | *HARRY'S APT. BLDG/H's LIVINGROOM* | *INT* |
| SCENE NO. | SCENE NAME | INT. OR EXT. |
| *HARRY PLAYS SAX SOLO W/RECORD* | | *NIGHT* |
| DESCRIPTION | | DAY OR NIGHT |
| | | *3/8* |
| | | PAGE COUNT |

| CAST Red (1301-2-3) | STUNTS Orange (1304) | EXTRAS/ATMOSPHERE Green (1322) |
|---|---|---|
| *HARRY* | | |
| | EXTRAS/SILENT BITS Yellow (1321) | |
| SPECIAL EFFECTS Blue (2300) | PROPS Violet (2500) | VEHICLES/ANIMALS Pink (2600/4500) |
| | - *1 LARGE HOMEMADE LOUDSPEAKER (OLD-FASHIONED) ALTEC A-500* <br> - *STRAIGHT-BACK WOODEN CHAIR* <br> - *SAXOPHONE* | |
| WARDROBE Circle (3400) | MAKE-UP/HAIR Asterisk (3500) | SOUND EFFECTS/MUSIC Brown (5100,5300,5400) <br> *JAZZ RECORD W/ APPLAUSE* |
| SPECIAL EQUIPMENT Box | PRODUCTION NOTES <br> - *TECH ADVISOR-SAX* <br> - *MAKE-UP, HARRY SWEATING* | |

© 1984 Lone Eagle Productions, Inc.

37

| CODE — BREAKDOWN SHEETS/STRIPS<br>Day Ext. — Yellow<br>Night Ext. — Green<br>Day Int. — White<br>Night Int. — Blue<br>Numbers refer to<br>budget categories | **SCRIPT**<br>**BREAKDOWN SHEET** | _MARCH 22, 1984_<br>DATE |

49

| PRODUCTION COMPANY<br>_49_ | PRODUCTION TITLE/NO.<br>_HARRY'S APT. BLDG._ | BREAKDOWN PAGE NO.<br>_EXT._ |
| SCENE NO. | SCENE NAME | INT. OR EXT. |
| _HARRY EXITS BLDG. + PASSES DEMOLITION CREW_ | | _DAY_ |
| DESCRIPTION | | DAY OR NIGHT |
| | | _2/8_ |
| | | PAGE COUNT |

| **CAST**<br>Red (1301-2-3)<br><br>_HARRY_ | **STUNTS**<br>Orange (1304) | **EXTRAS/ATMOSPHERE**<br>Green (1322)<br>_CONSTRUCTION CREW (25)_<br>_15 N.D. EXTRAS_ |
| | **EXTRAS/SILENT BITS**<br>Yellow (1321) | |
| **SPECIAL EFFECTS**<br>Blue (2300) | **PROPS**<br>Violet (2500)<br>_BUS STOP SIGN_<br>_BENCH_ | **VEHICLES/ANIMALS**<br>Pink (2600/4500) |
| **WARDROBE**<br>Circle (3400) | **MAKE-UP/HAIR**<br>Asterisk (3500) | **SOUND EFFECTS/MUSIC**<br>Brown (5100,5300,5400)<br>_DEMOLITION SOUNDS_ |
| **SPECIAL EQUIPMENT**<br>Box<br>_BUILDING/CONSTRUCTION CREW - TRUCKS, JACK HAMMERS, CRANE?_ | **PRODUCTION NOTES** | |

©1984 Lone Eagle Productions, Inc.

38

CODE — BREAKDOWN SHEETS/STRIPS
Day Ext. — Yellow
Night Ext. — Green
Day Int. — White
Night Int. — Blue
Numbers refer to
budget categories

# SCRIPT
# BREAKDOWN SHEET

MARCH 22, 1984
DATE

50
BREAKDOWN PAGE NO.

| PRODUCTION COMPANY | PRODUCTION TITLE/NO. | |
|---|---|---|
| 50 | INDUSTRIAL AREA/HARRY'S WHSE. | EXT |
| **SCENE NO.** | **SCENE NAME** | INT. OR EXT. |
| HARRY ENTERS WAREHOUSE ELEVATOR | | DAY |
| **DESCRIPTION** | | DAY OR NIGHT |
| | | 2/8 |
| | | PAGE COUNT |

| CAST
Red (1301-2-3)

HARRY | STUNTS
Orange (1304) | EXTRAS/ATMOSPHERE
Green (1322)

25 WAREHOUSE TYPES |
|---|---|---|
| | **EXTRAS/SILENT BITS**
Yellow (1321) | |
| **SPECIAL EFFECTS**
Blue (2300) | **PROPS**
Violet (2500)

ASSORTED BOXES | **VEHICLES/ANIMALS**
Pink (2600/4500)

TRUCKS (DOUBLE PARKED) |
| **WARDROBE**
Circle (3400) | **MAKE-UP/HAIR**
Asterisk (3500) | **SOUND EFFECTS/MUSIC**
Brown (5100,5300,5400) |
| **SPECIAL EQUIPMENT**
Box

FREIGHT TRAIN, FORK LIFTS,
HAND TRUCKS, ETC.
INDUSTRIAL ELEVATOR
OR ELEVATOR IN WAREHOUSE
W/ BUTTON | **PRODUCTION NOTES**

TECHNICAL ADVISOR-
INDUSTRIAL ELEVATOR | |

© 1984 Lone Eagle Productions, Inc.

CODE — BREAKDOWN SHEETS/STRIPS
Day Ext. — Yellow
Night Ext. — Green
Day Int. — White
Night Int. — Blue
Numbers refer to
budget categories

# SCRIPT
# BREAKDOWN SHEET

DATE: MARCH 22, 1984

BREAKDOWN PAGE NO.: 51

| PRODUCTION COMPANY 51 | PRODUCTION TITLE/NO. HARRY'S WAREHOUSE – OFFICE | INT. |

SCENE NO.: 51
SCENE NAME
INT. OR EXT.: INT.

DESCRIPTION: HARRY + STANLEY TALK
DAY OR NIGHT: DAY

PAGE COUNT: 6/8

**CAST** Red (1301-2-3)
HARRY
STANLEY

**STUNTS** Orange (1304)

**EXTRAS/ATMOSPHERE** Green (1322)

**EXTRAS/SILENT BITS** Yellow (1321)

**SPECIAL EFFECTS** Blue (2300)

**PROPS** Violet (2500)
BENCHES
ELECTRONIC SURVEILLANCE EQUIPMENT
CABINETS + SHELVES
OLD SOFA
MAGAZINE
THREE PROP. TAPE RECORDERS
MANILA ENVELOPE – SEVERAL PHOTOS

**VEHICLES/ANIMALS** Pink (2600/4500)

**WARDROBE** Circle (3400)

**MAKE-UP/HAIR** Asterisk (3500)

**SOUND EFFECTS/MUSIC** Brown (5100,5300,5400)

**SPECIAL EQUIPMENT** Box

**PRODUCTION NOTES**
1. TECH. ADVISOR – SURVEILLANCE EQUIP.
2. COAT/ HARRY
3. SEVERAL PHOTOS OF ANN + MARK
   8X10 B+W TAKEN FROM SURVEILLANCE SCENE. IF
   SHOT FIRST — OTHERWISE MUST BE STAGED
   (SCHEDULE STILL SESSION)

© 1984 Lone Eagle Productions, Inc.

# V

# THE PRODUCTION BOARD

Now that you have completed your breakdown sheets, we can move on to the next step:

## Creating the Production Board

In order to schedule your film project, you must be able to look at all the variables and re-arrange their order easily. You will need to do this not only at the beginning of your project when you are estimating length and cost, but also during the actual shooting of the project. As you will see in later chapters, it is not unusual for a schedule to be re-arranged during shooting to accommodate a change. These changes come from your PARAMETER GUIDES (see Chapter VI). If you were trying to schedule your project using only the breakdown sheets, you would have quite a cumbersome task in trying to look at all the sheets simultaneously. To facilitate scheduling, only the most pertinent information is listed on a small, color-coded PRODUC-TION STRIP which is stored on the PRODUCTION BOARD. This board can be handled and transported easily, and can be almost any length you wish. Commercially produced strips and strip boards are either 15" high or 18-1/4" high. We recommend that you use the 15" strips and board as they can easily be photocopied. The 18-1/4" strips are too long and photocopying would require too much cutting and pasting. When you choose which height board you are going to work with, try to purchase all the strips from one manufacturer. Although they are all basically the same, the lines on the strips do vary from manufacturer to manufacturer and if you mix them, they won't line up.

Production boards are constructed from different materials—cardboard or wood are the usual choices. Cardboard boards are the least expensive and most commonly used. Both the cardboard and wooden boards come in varying sizes according to the number of PANELS. One panel holds approximately 25 strips and is about 10 inches wide. The average feature film project would require a board approximately 6 to 8 panels in length. THE CONVERSATION will require at least 8 panels.

If you find that you are going to be using a Strip Board on a fairly regular basis, it might be advisable to have one built (or build it yourself). It will cost from $100 on up depending on how many panels, what materials you use and how elaborate you want to get. At this writing, an eight-panel cardboard board now costs about $85, so you might want to consider acquiring your own board sooner than later. If you do decide to have one made, make sure that the working surface (the area where you will place your strips) is slightly convex. Your strips will stay in place much better than in the standard flat surface board because of the slight tension placed on them due to the design. Dependable hinges and a good leather carrying handle are also good ideas.

You will be able to buy strips and boards from the following companies:

**Gilbert Mandelik** (handcrafted wood boards only)
1650 N. Kings Road
Los Angeles, CA 90069
213/654-5524

**Peter Griffin**
Hollywood Production Boards
7469 Melrose Avenue #29
Los Angeles, CA 90046
213/651-4220

**Production Boards by Jack Cash**
650 N. Bronson
Los Angeles, CA 90004
213/463-5885

**Enterprise Stationers**
7401 Sunset Blvd.
Los Angeles, CA 90046
213/876-3530

**Earl Hays Press**
10707 Sherman Way
Sun Valley, CA 91352
213/765-0700

**F & B Ceco**
315 West 43rd Street
New York, New York 10036
212/974-4600

## Materials

1 bundle of each of the following color strips: blue, green, white, yellow, fluorescent pink, and either red or orange.

# Film Scheduling

1 bundle strips which are white at the top and black on the bottom.

2 Headers (Head Boards).

2 or 3 black pens which will not smear. Ball points work very well as do "Penstix" (Alvin - EEF). You can find these at good art supply stores. Their ink is very good (also indelible) and reproduces well on copy machines. We do not recommend using regular felt tips as they tend to smear.

Bottles of "white-out" fluid in colors to match the strips.

1 Production Strip Board - about 8 panels.

1 two-panel Strip Board which will serve as your Holding Board.

Several different colors of small adhesive "dots"—suggest red, black, green, etc. These could be used to mark scenes which take place in another city, or in the case of THE CONVERSA-TION, we will use them to mark the scenes in which the dialogue has been pre-recorded.

## Head Board

To begin making your Production Board, start with the Head Board or Header. Refer to the example in this chapter. The Header will be the index for all the other information which you will put on the strips to eventually make your Production Board. Since every manufacturer of strips and head has its own particular listing of information, you may find that you will have to re-arrange the order to suit your needs.

44

Your Head Board lines should read as follows:

**Line 1** - Blank (in case you need to mark anything extraordinary such as Second Unit, Change in Time Period, Material to be shot in another country/state/city, etc. This is a good place for the "dots" which we mentioned earlier.

**Line 2** - Day or Night

**Line 3** - Breakdown Page Number

**Line 4** - Exterior or Interior

**Line 5** - Scene Number

Go on down the strip and fill in the appropriate information next to, **Title, Director, Producer, Assistant Director,** etc. Fill in **Prod. Mgr.** and the appropriate name in the space which follows.

Next to **Script Dated** put in the date the script was written. Usually, you will find this on the title page of the script. If there is none, write in the date on which you complete the production board. It is very likely that the script will undergo some rewrites which may necessitate changing the board. Dating the board and the script will make it easier to identify later on. Mark the date only on the header—not on the individual strips themselves.

The next group of lines is reserved for the cast members. Go back to your breakdown sheets and, on a separate piece of paper entitled **Cast,** list each character and the number of the scene in which the actor appears. Don't just make a "tick" mark, list the actual scene number. You will need this information later on. List every actor/actress who says one word (including voice-overs), and then count the total number of scenes for each character. The actor/actress who has the most number of scenes is #1, the actor/actress with the second number of scenes is #2, and so forth. The only time you will make an exception is out of respect to a well-known actor who may have a smaller part. In THE CONVERSATION, Harry Caul is #1, Ann is #2, Mark is #3, and Mr. C is #4. You know that Mr. C has fewer scenes than either Stanley or Paul, but yet he is listed in fourth position. Well, when THE CONVERSATION was made, Robert Duvall, who played Mr. C., was much more well-known than John Cazale who played Stanley, and Michael Higgins who played Paul. Again, if you have a hesitation about which actor should be listed first, it is a good idea to check with the producer (or director) so that there aren't any unintentional slights.

If you find that you have more than 25 speaking parts, you have a choice—either double them up or use a separate head board. In the case of THE CONVERSATION, we chose to double up as the smaller speaking parts were not all in the same scenes. Don't list the actor/actress' names as that can change. List only the name of the character.

**Note:** Never use the bottom ten spaces of the Head Board for Characters' names — this will be explained later.

Since we have more than 25 speaking parts, we have listed only 16 of the most important and then split the column in two. Take the time to white out the numbers which you will not need and to write in the correct number—now. Once a number is assigned to a character, that is his/her number throughout the entire production board and later on in the shooting schedule. Some production managers alternate red and black ink so that they will stand out. Other production managers list the minor characters' names in a different color ink and then double them up all the way on the board. We prefer not to rely on different color inks as you won't be able to differentiate them when they are photocopied (unless it's a color copier). If you find that you are going to be working on a very long project—a mini-series, for example, then we urge you to use as many head boards as you need. Fill in only the **Character** section of the head board, and place it to the right of the main head board.

In the bottom ten spaces, we shall list other elements which will be specially scheduled. Some of these and their corresponding code letters are:

| | |
|---|---|
| **Music** | Ⓜ |
| **Special Effects** | (SFX) |
| **Special Equipment** | (SE) |
| **Animals** | Ⓐ |
| **Extras (*actual number*)** | (#) |
| **Rain** | Ⓡ |

You will find that you will develop your own symbols for these. There are others which you will think of. Establish your own system and legend. Always put a circle around these elements to help draw your attention to them. In the case of Extras, it is essential that you circle the number as you may become confused with the character number.

## Filling in the Strips

When beginning to fill in the strips, it is wise to use your two-panel Holding Board. You can also use a large flat table, but chances are your strips will get out of order and everything won't be lined up properly. Finish all the strips for one sequence before transferring them over to your large board. Keep your strips in chronological order—don't try to jump ahead.

| Day or Nite | | | |
|---|---|---|---|
| BREAK DOWN PAGE # | | | |
| EXTERIOR OR INTERIOR | | | |
| SCENE # | | | |
| | | | |
| | | | |
| | | | |
| Title THE CONVERSATION | | | |
| Director FRANCIS COPPOLA | | | |
| Producer | | | |
| Asst. Director | | | |
| PROD'N MGR CLARK PAYLOW | | | |
| NO. OF PAGES | | | |
| Character | Artist | | No. |
| HARRY CAUL | | | 1 |
| ANN | | | 2 |
| MARK | | | 3 |
| MR. C. | | | 4 |
| STANLEY | | | 5 |
| PAUL MEYERS | | | 6 |
| MARTIN | | | 7 |
| WILLIAM P. MORGAN | | | 8 |
| MEREDITH | | | 9 |
| MILLARD | | | 10 |
| MRS. GOETNER | | | 11 |
| RON KELLER | | | 12 |
| MRS. CORSITTO | | | 13 |
| BOB | | | 14 |
| BOB'S WIFE | | | 15 |
| AMY | | | 16 |
| LURLEEN | | | 17 |
| MALE SEC'Y | 18 | TONY | 19 |
| MALE RECEPT. | 20 | MIME | 21 |
| YOUNG MAN | 22 | YOUNG WOMAN | 23 |
| SHOPPER #1 | 24 | SHOPPER #2 | 25 |
| SHOPPER #3 | 26 | LAUNDRY LADY | 27 |
| #27's Little Boy | 28 | WOMAN #1-ELEV | 29 |
| WOMAN #2-ELEV. | 30 | MAN IN ELEVATOR | 31 |
| DEMO MAN | 32 | SPEAKER | 33 |
| MAN IN BOOTH | 34 | YOUNG DRIVER | 35 |
| MOTEL CLERK | 36 | BUS DRIVER #1 | 37 |
| BUS DRIVER #2 | 38 | MCNAUGHT | 39 |
| ANNC'R/PA SYST. | 40 | TEL. OPER #1 | 41 |
| CHROME DOMEVO | 42 | WOMAN IN RRM | 43 |
| TEL. OPER. #2 | 44 | MAN #2 IN BOOTH | 45 |
| | | | |
| MUSIC : (M) | | CARS : (C) | |
| SPECIAL EQUIPMENT : (SE) | | | |
| ANIMALS : A | | | |
| EXTRAS: (#) | | | |
| | | | |

Your project may not have as many scenes (or shots) as THE CONVERSATION has. One hundred fifty to two hundred scenes would be considered fairly normal for a 100 - 120 page script. Usually, we recommend that you put each scene on a separate strip. In the case of THE CONVERSATION, however, we are dealing with over 300 scenes, many of which are just different angles of the same scene. In this case it is perfectly alright to combine scenes onto one strip, so long as all the information is exactly the same and represents only a change in angle. If you are at all hesitant, then put the information on separate strips. Be aware that if you do combine shots onto one strip, you may have to go back later and make individual strips if something changes in a revision.

Now you can begin making your strips. As mentioned earlier, the production strips are also color-coded to correspond to the breakdown sheets: YELLOW = Day Exterior, WHITE = Day Interior, GREEN = Night Exterior, BLUE = Night Interior. Look at your first breakdown sheet—Yellow, which tells you the shot is a Day Exterior. Take your yellow strip and place it in the holding board to the right of the head board, making sure that the lines line up evenly. Don't start writing yet.

Now, look back at your breakdown sheets. Scenes 1 - 11 all take place in Union Square, so perhaps they could all be listed on one strip. Looking a little closer, we see that Scenes 10 and 11 are views from the rooftop overlooking the Square, so let's break them out. Look at the rest of the Scenes 1 - 9. Go back and re-read the scenes in the script. We don't discover Harry Caul until Scene 3 and don't meet Ann and Mark until Scene 9. From the way it is written, however, it is very possible that all three of these characters could be seen in the background and just not identified until later scenes. As the location, time of day, number of extras, etc., are all the same, we have chosen to combine Scenes 1 - 9 onto one strip. When you do this, make sure that you go through all the corresponding breakdown sheets and transfer all the pertinent information from each sheet onto the strip.

Beginning at the top of the strip, these scenes take place in the daytime, so, if it isn't already pre-printed on your yellow strip, mark "D." These are breakdown sheets 1-9 and they are an EXT. The scenes are 1-9. In the space corresponding to the space marked Script Dated on the head board, mark the PAGE COUNT. Go through the first 9 breakdown sheets and total the number of pages you have. It should be 3-1/8. (If you are not sure, go back to your script to double-check.)

Then go through and fill in the characters which appear. Whenever a character appears in a scene (or group of shots) mark the number of the character (e.g., #2 for Ann) in the corresponding space. Do not just mark an "X" or "√".

In the event that two characters who are sharing the same space have to appear in the same scene, just move one of the characters up or down one space or divide the space with a slash (/). This probably won't happen too often.

Now, go through the first nine breakdown sheets and mark every character who appears in any of the nine scenes. Your strip will have the following marked on it: #1 (Harry Caul), #2 (Ann), #3 (Mark), #21 (Mime), #22 (Young Man), #23 (Young Woman), Ⓜ(Music), ⓈⒺ(Special Equipment) and ⑫⑤ (Extras). When you have completed all the information to be listed across the strip horizontally, turn your board 1/4 turn sideways. In the blank space at the top of the strip between "Scene #" and "Page Count" write out the location of the scene, e.g., **Union Square.** In the space at the very bottom of the strip, write out a brief description of the action. You will get this information from the breakdown sheets. Don't use full sentences. The shorter the better. *"Surveillance"* is how we describe these scenes.

Now that you understand how to complete your first strip, fill it in and leave it in the holding board. Proceed with the next strip, following the same steps which we outlined above.

From time to time, you will see that an actor/actress is mentioned in one scene and it is implied that he/she should be in the next scene. If you are unclear as to whether the actor/actress should be in the scene and you haven't been able to ask the director, mark the actor/actress as appearing in the scene and put a question mark beside the number. Two good examples of this are Scene 34 - Exterior Bus, and Scene 35 - Interior Bus. In Scene 34, Harry is not mentioned, but he appears in Scene 35. We will put a "?" beside his number (#1) in Scene 34, as we are not sure whether he will be seen by the camera or not. Mark this, and any other questions you will have, on your list of questions to ask the director and/or producer.

THE CONVERSATION uses footage more than one time. This doesn't mean that you have to shoot it more than once, only that it has to be scheduled and accounted for. In order to differentiate between previously shot material and new material, we have put a small horizontal line in the top-most square of the appropriate strip. We could also use small dots, or any other mark which you prefer which is clear, distinct and uniform.

Even though you have gone through the breakdown sheets, it is a good idea to have your marked-up script handy so that you

51

**Title:** THE CONVERSATION
**Director:** FRANCIS COPPOLA
**Producer:**
**Asst. Director:**
**Prod'n Mgr:** CLARK PAYLOW

| | | | | | | | | | | | | | | | | | |
|---|---|---|---|---|---|---|---|---|---|---|---|---|---|---|---|---|---|
| Day or Nite | D | D | D | D | D | D | D | D | D | D | D | D | D | D | D | D | D |
| BREAK DOWN PAGE # | 1-9 | 10-11 | 12 | 13 | 14-16 | 17 | 18 | 19-22 | 23-24 | 25-26 | 27 | 28 | 29 | 30 | 31 | 32 | 33 |
| EXTERIOR OR INTERIOR | E | E | I | I | I | E | E | E | E | E | I | E | I | E | E | E | E |
| SCENE | 1-9 | 10-11 | 12 | 13 | 14-16 | 17 | 18 | 19-22 | 23-24 | 25-26 | 27 | 28 | 29 | 30 | 31 | 32 | 33 |
| Location | UNION SQUARE | UNION SQUARE | PANEL VAN TRUCK | STREET/VAN TRUCK | PANEL VAN TRUCK | EIFFEL TOWER/TOP | EIFFEL TOWER/TOP | UNION SQUARE | OFFICE BLDG. WINDOW | EIFFEL TOWER/TOP | PANEL VAN TRUCK | UNION SQUARE | PANEL VAN TRUCK | PANEL VAN TRUCK | EIFFEL TOWER/TOP | OFFICE BLDG WINDOW | UNION SQUARE |
| NO. OF PAGES | 3 3/8 | 3/8 | 4/8 | 1/8 | 2 1/8 | 2/8 | 2/8 | 1/8 | 6/8 | 5/8 | 1 2/8 | 2/8 | 5/8 | 1/8 | 1/8 | 1/8 | 1/8 |

| Character / Artist | No. | | | | | | | | | | | | | | | | | |
|---|---|---|---|---|---|---|---|---|---|---|---|---|---|---|---|---|---|---|
| HARRY CAUL | 1 | 1 | | 1 | | 1 | | | | | | 1 | 2 | 1 | | | | |
| ANN | 2 | 2 | 2 | 2 | . | | | | 2 | 2 | 2 | 2 | 20^v | 3 | | | | |
| MARK | 3 | 3 | | 3 | | | 30^v | 3 | 3 | 3 | 3 | 30^v | | | | | | |
| MR. C. | 4 | | | | | | | | | | | | | | | | | |
| STANLEY | 5 | | | 5 | | 5 | | | | | | 5 | | 5 | | | | |
| PAUL MEYERS | 6 | 6 | | | | | | | 6 | 6 | | 6 | | | | | | |
| MARTIN | 7 | | | | | | | | | | | | | | | | | |
| WILLIAM P. MORAN | 8 | | | | | | | | | | | | | | | | | |
| MEREDITH | 9 | | | | | | | | | | | | | | | | | |
| MILLARD | 10 | | | | | | | | | | | | | | | | | |
| MRS. GOETNER | 11 | | | | | | | | | | | | | | | | | |
| RON. KELLER | 12 | | | | | | | | | | | | | | | | | |
| MRS. CORSITTO | 13 | | | | | | | | | | | | | | | | | |
| BOB | 14 | | | | | | | | | | | | | | | | | |
| BOB'S WIFE | 15 | | | | | | | | | | | | | | | | | |
| AMY | 16 | | | | | | | | | | | | | | | | | |
| LURLEEN | 17 | | | | | | | | | | | | | | | | | |
| MALE SEC'Y — (M) TONY | 19 | | | | | | | | | | | | | | | | | |
| MALE RECEPT (20) — MIME | 21 | 21 | | | | | | | 21 | 21 | 21 | | | | | | | 21 |
| YOUNG MAN (22) — YOUNG WOMAN | 23 | 22 | | | | | | | | | | | | | | | | |
| SHOPPER #1 (24) — SHOPPER #2 | 25 | 23 | | | | | | | 24 | | | | | | | | | |
| SHOPPER #3 (26) — LAUNDRY LADY | 27 | | | | | | | | 25 | | | | | | | | | |
| #27's Little Boy (28) — WOMAN #1-ELEV | 29 | | | | | | | | 26 | | | | | | | | | |
| WOMAN #2-ELEV (30) — MAN IN ELEVATOR | 31 | | | | | | | | | | | | | | | | | |
| DEMO MAN (32) — SPEAKER | 33 | | | | | | | | (M) | | | | | | | | | |
| MAN IN BOOTH (34) — YOUNG DRIVER | 35 | | | | | | | | (SE) | | | | | | | | | |
| MOTEL CLERK (36) — BUS DRIVER #1 | 37 | | (C) | | | | (SE) | | (125) | | | (C) | | | (C) | (SE) | | |
| BUS DRIVER #2 (38) — MCNAUGHT | 39 | | (SE) | | | | (50#) | | (50#)(125) | (50#)(25) | (C) | | | | | | | |
| ANN'C'R/PA SYST (40) — TEL.OPER. #1 | 41 | (M) | (25) | | | | ROOF# | | (50#/125) | (50#/25) | (SE) | | | | | | (SE) | (SE)(25) |
| CHROME DOME VO (42) — WOMAN IN RRM | 43 | (C) | | (C) | (C) | (C) | | | | | | (125) | | | | | | |
| TEL.OPER. #2 (44) — MAN #2 IN BOOTH | 45 | (SE) | (SE) | | (SE) | | | | (SE) | (125) | | | (125) | | | | | |

MUSIC: (M)   CARS: (C)
SPECIAL EQUIPMENT: (SE)
ANIMALS: (A)
EXTRAS: (#)

Column scene descriptions (left to right):
1. SURVEILLANCE
2. CLOSE-UP-ANN
3. SURVEILLANCE OF COUPLE
4. GIRLS FIX MAKE-UP
5. DISCUSS SURVEILLANCE
6. SURVEILLANCE FROM ROOF
7. THEY WALK & TALK
8. THEY ARE TAILED
9. THEY DISCOVER PAUL
10. SURVEILLANCE NEAR BONGOS
11. THEY PAY PAUL, LISTEN
12. COUPLE PARTS
13. HARRY MAKES A JOKE
14. LAUGHTER FROM WITHIN
15. MAN PUTS EQUIP. AWAY
16. MAN PACKS EQUIP.
17. MUSICIANS PACKUP

| D/N | Scene | I/E | Scene | Location | Pages | Action |
|---|---|---|---|---|---|---|
| D | 34 | E | 34 | ELECTRIC BUS | 1/8 | BUS MOVES ALONG |
| D | 35 | I | 35 | ELECTRIC BUS | 2/8 | HE EXITS BUS |
| D | 36-37 | I | 36-37 | HARRY'S NEIGHBORHOOD | 2/8 | CROSSES STREET, GOES PARK |
| D | 38 | I | 38 | NEIGHBORHOOD MARKET | 1/8 | SHOPS FOR DINNER |
| D | 39 | I | 39 | NEIGHBORHOOD LAUNDRY | 5/8 | PICKS UP LAUNDRY/MUSIC |
| D | 40 | I | 40 | HARRY'S APT. BLDG - FOYER | 3/8 | CHECKS MAIL, GREETS NEIGHBOR |
| D | 41 | I | 41 | HARRY'S APARTMENT | 1 | HARRY CALLS APT. MANAGER |
| N | 42 | I | 42 | HARRY'S APT. KITCHENETTE | 1 7/8 | DISTURBED BY TENANTS |
| N | 43 | I | 43 | HARRY'S APT. BLDG. FLOOR HALL | 3/8 | BOB TALKS TO HARRY |
| N | 44 | E | 44 | HARRY'S APT. | 3 5/8 | BIRTHDAY PARTY |
| N | 45 | I | 45 | ELECTRIC BUS | 1/8 | EXITS BUS, ENTERS BLDG |
| N | 46 | I | 46 | AMY'S BLDG.-HALL-APT. | 2/8 | CLIMBS STAIRS, ENTERS APT |
| N | 47 | I | 47 | AMY'S APT. | 5 3/8 | HARRY VISITS AMY |
| N | 48 | E | 48 | HARRY'S APT. | 3/8 | HARRY PLAYS JAX |
| D | 49 | E | 49 | HARRY'S APT. BLDG. | 1/8 | HARRY EXITS BUILDING |
| D | 50 | I | 50 | HARRY'S WARE HOUSE | 2/8 | ENTERS A'S WAREHOUSE |
| D | 51-57 | E | 51-57 | H'S WAREHOUSE WORK AREA | 2 4/8 | DISCUSS CONVENTION/WORK |
| D | 58 | I | 58 | UNION SQUARE | 5/8 | [REPEAT OPENING - SEE SCENE 9] |
| D | 59-61 | E | 59-61 | H'S WAREHOUSE WORK AREA | 3/8 | C.U. EQUIP / HARRY |
| D | 62 | E | 62 | UNION SQUARE | 3/8 | [REPEAT OPENING] |
| D | 63 | I | 63 | H'S WAREHOUSE WORK AREA | 4/8 | LISTENS TO CONVERSATION |
| D | 64 | E | 64 | UNION SQUARE | 1/8 | [REPEAT OPENING - SCN #9] |
| D | 65 | I | 65 | A'S WAREHOUSE WORK AREA | 2/8 | PLAYS IT AGAIN |
| D | 66 | E | 66 | UNION SQUARE | 3/8 | [REPEAT ORIGINAL OPENING] |
| D | 67 | I | 67 | H'S WAREHOUSE WORK AREA | 3 2/8 | HARRY & STANLEY DISAGREE |
| D | 68 | E | 68 | UNION SQUARE | 7/8 | THEY TALK |
| D | 69-70 | I | 69-70 | H'S WAREHOUSE WORK AREA | 4/8 | WORKS ON FILTERING CONVERSATION |

Strip / cast markings (as noted on board):

- Cast "1": appears in scenes 34 (1?), 35, 36-37, 38, 39, 41, 42, 43, 44, 45, 46, 47, 48, 49, 50, 51-57, 58, 59-61, 62, 65, 67, 69-70
- Cast "2": 51-57 (2 v.o.), 58 (2), 62 (2), 63 (2 v.o.), 65 (2 v.o.), 66 (2), 67 (2 v.o.), 68 (2), 69-70 (2 v.o.)
- Cast "3": 51-57 (3 v.o.), 58 (3), 59-61 (3 v.o.), 62 (3), 63 (3 v.o.), 65 (3 v.o.), 66 (3), 67 (3 v.o.), 68 (3), 69-70 (3 v.o.)
- Cast "5": 51-57 (5), 63 (5), 67 (5)
- Cast "11": 40, 43
- Cast "12": 41, 42, 43
- Cast "13": 41, 43
- Cast "14": 41, 42, 43
- Cast "15": 41, 42, 43
- Cast "16": 46 (16 v.o.), 47 (16)
- Cast "21": 67
- Cast "27", "28": 38
- "SE" markings: 69-70, and several scenes

can double check each element. It takes a little more time, but it is worth catching those few possible mistakes up front.

**Caution!** Make sure that when you combine scenes (or shots) you do not violate any of the rules (*day/night, interior/exterior, etc*). Sometimes deciding whether two scenes should be put on the same strip is very, very tricky. If in doubt, do not combine scenes.

Keeping all this in mind, go ahead and complete your strips for THE CONVERSATION. When you have finished making all your strips, check your board against the one on the fold out production board. It is a good idea once you have all your strips done to number the strips on the back so that you will know if one is missing.

# VI
## PARAMETER FACTORS

In deciding what to schedule when, certain factors must be considered. Here, then in order of their priority, is the list.

### Parameter Factors
1) Locations
2) Cast Members
3) Day/Night Shooting
4) Exteriors/Interiors
5) Shooting In Sequence
6) Child Actors
7) Changes in Time Periods
8) Time of the Year
9) Weather Conditions
10) Special Effects & Stunts
11) Second Camera and/or Second
     Unit
12) Special Equipment
13) Geography of Locations
14) Miscellaneous Factors

1)  **Locations:** Unless absolutely necessary, you do not want to go back to a location once you have finished with it.

Certain locations will only allow you to film on certain days of the week during certain hours. On a recent film, the production manager had the problem of trying to schedule a scene in the New York Public Library. The Library's policy is to allow filming on the day that it is closed to the public - Thursday. The crew had four weeks in New York to complete shooting. Two of the possible Thursdays were Christmas Eve and New Year's Eve. Because the Library was going to be closed on the two Fridays (Christmas and New Year's), they decided to stay open on those two Thursdays. So, within a four week schedule, there were only two possible days to shoot the scenes in the New York Public Library the Thursday before (Dec. 17th) and the Thursday after (January 6). Suddenly, what started out as an ordinary scene became a major scheduling problem. It took a bit of juggling, but it finally worked out.

2)   **Cast Members:** For economic reasons, it is best to try to work an actor's schedule so that you have the fewest number of necessary work days and the fewest number of HOLDING DAYS in between. This also works to the actor's advantage, as he is free to accept other employment as soon as his part is finished.

There are many strict rules concerning actors—we have even separated CHILD ACTORS and given them their own category (#5). Before starting to schedule, it is best to get a copy of the latest edition of the Screen Actors Guild contract and read it. Here are a few key rules which you must know and which will affect your schedule.

a) **Always Up-Grade, Never Down-Grade:** During the production of a project, an actor can always be up-graded, never down-graded. For example, an Ex-

56

tra can move up to a Speaking Part (DAY PLAYER), but a Day Player can never drop to an Extra. A Day Player can be put on a weekly contract, but never vice-versa. And, once that up-grade has been made, it is not reversible on the show.

b) **Drop-And-Pick-Up:** An actor may be "dropped" and "picked-up" only once during a show. Suppose you have a situation where you need a particular actor for three days at the beginning of the schedule and then another five days later on. Unless there are ten free calendar days (with the actor working again on the 11th) you will have to pay the actor for the holding days — the days in-between. The actors are paid at full rate. Suppose that you need this same actor for the time specified above, and an additional four days even later on. If your schedule permits you to drop and pick-up the actor between the first three days and the second five, you will have to pay for all the holding days between the second time he works and the third time.

In some instances, you may find it is less expensive to keep the actor and pay for the holding days because of other **PARAMETER FACTORS** which if rearranged, could result in higher costs to the film.

c) **Run-Of-Show Deal:** In looking over the list of actors and scene numbers which you used to determine which actor was #1, #2 etc., you may find that an actor is in so many scenes that it makes more sense to have him around for the entire show. This kind of deal is called a RUN-OF-SHOW DEAL and pays the actor a certain amount for a certain number of weeks' work—no matter how many or how few days he works within those weeks. Harry Caul is an example of an actor who should have a run-of-show deal. If the project involves a well-known actor, then the producers have probably already made this deal. This will eliminate this actor as a major scheduling problem. You may find that it is the smaller parts which prove to be the most difficult scheduling problems.

Run-of-show deals never become drop-and-pick-up.

d) **Special Clauses:** Some actors have special clauses in their contracts which determine the amount of time they may work during the day; or that they cannot start before such-and-such a time or must end work by such-and-such a time. If the actor is hired under these conditions, then the rules must be adhered to.

3)    **Day And Night Shooting:** When you lay out your locations, keep in mind that you cannot schedule a full "day's" work after finishing a full "night's" work. Most of the Unions and Guilds have very strict rules concerning TURN-AROUND TIME—the minimum number of time-off a person must have before coming back to work. For example, during the week—an actor must have twelve hours off from the time he leaves the set and returns to work. Travel to and from the location must be added in if the location is not considered a local location. He must have 58 uninterrupted hours from the completion of Friday's work to Monday's work. If Friday was a night shoot, then the actors and crew will need a minimum amount of uninterrupted free time before they may report back to

work. Any violation of these hours results in having to pay a PENALTY—very expensive and should be avoided unless absolutely necessary. Each Union/Guild has its own rules, and as you guessed, not too many of them are similar.

As for shooting at night, it is best to try to schedule your night work on a Friday (if working a five-day week) or even block out an entire week for night work. Switching from day shooting to night shooting causes the same kind of jet lag and slowness which you experience when flying across the country. Don't expect to accomplish the same amount of work at night.

4)  **Exteriors/Interiors:** It is a good idea to always shoot your exteriors before moving inside. Although Production Managers try to control as many of the variables as possible, there is one variable that cannot be controlled—sun, or lack of it. It is much easier, except in certain unusual circumstances, to DRESS windows so as to give the appearance of night when filming a night interior in the day time than it is to create the illusion of night when filming outside.

5)  **Shooting in Sequence:** Whenever possible, try to shoot all of the scenes in one location in sequential order. If an actor is required to build to an emotional point at the end of the scene, it will be easier for the actor and for the director if the sequence is shot in order.

Sometimes, however, it is just not possible to shoot in sequence. Take a location which has many windows facing west on one side of the room. If you were trying to film in that location in winter, you would find that the light in the room would change almost continuously and that you would lose your light very quickly. Because of the nature of the location, you are going to be forced to shoot all the scenes facing the window at one time of day and all the other ones either before or after. This problem could add extra days to the location and possibly to the schedule.

6) **Child Actors:** As we mentioned under Cast Members, rules for child actors are quite strict. Depending on the age of the child (or children), a TEACHER or WELFARE WORKER may be necessary. The hours a child actor may work and under what conditions are very strict. Make sure that you consult with the Screen Actors Guild before trying to schedule a child actor.

7) **Changes In Time Period:** If a script is set in any other time period but the present day, a certain amount of time must be spent to ensure that all the elements fit the period of time you are depicting. It looks out of place to have a 1930's movie with 1980's streetlights. Or, a futuristic film with everyday street clothes. Special make-up and wardrobe may be needed; sets have to be specially constructed, etc. All this requires time—time which must be allotted and scheduled.

In THE REINCARNATION OF PETER PROUD, the house (location) had to be shown in two different time periods—thirty years apart. In the present day scenes, the house had to be shown in a state of disrepair, almost decay. The paint was faded and chipped, and dust-covered cloths were on the furniture. It had to look as if no one had lived there for many years. In the flashback scenes (1940's), the house had to look brand new. The actress, Margot Kidder, played an elderly woman in present day and herself as a young woman in the flashbacks. Preparing both Ms. Kidder and the house were scheduling problems with which we had to contend. The house was shot first, present day, in its delapidated state. Then the shooting crew moved out and the art department moved in. About two weeks later, the shooting crew returned to a new-looking house, freshly painted inside and out. We shot the 1940's sequence. It required about two additional hours to make Ms. Kidder up to portray the elderly woman. On those days, we shot other scenes first so as not to always give Ms. Kidder an exceptionally early make-up call.

8)   **Time Of Year Filming:** As mentioned in an earlier example, winter months in the Northern Hemisphere mean less light. (Just the opposite in the Southern Hemisphere). As you move further north in winter, you will have less and less daylight. Take into consideration any unusual weather problems which you may encounter during the particular time of year—snow, rain, tornadoes, hurricanes, etc. In one part of California, the fog is so bad during some winter months that it is almost impossible to see. Knowing this will allow you to plan for the almost sure delays you will encounter. Call your local library, or better yet go there and check out the weather maps. Also, check *The Farmer's Almanac* (published annually every October).

9)   **Weather:** This factor can and does add more time to a winter picture where cold weather can affect not only movement of people and equipment, but also the film through the camera. Productions move more slowly in extreme cold weather—especially at night.

10)  **Special Effects & Stunts:** Depending on what is required for your project, it may require a lot of additional prepara-

tion time for Stunts and/or Special Effects. Especially on science-fiction films, many of the special effects will have to be created by computers. At this writing, there is one project which is about to begin eleven months of preparation and graphics work before they begin pre-production on the principal photography. The eleven months preparation is only for the computer generated images!

11) **Second Camera And/Or Second Unit:** SECOND CAMERA is an additional camera which shoots at the same time and on the same scene as the first camera. SECOND UNIT is an additional camera which shoots scenes other than what is being shot by the FIRST UNIT and does not include principal actors. A good way of compressing your time schedule is to use a second camera. However, it is not always the panacea that it appears to be. Some directors are not comfortable with a second camera. You will also need extra lighting as you will be lighting for two, not just one. Sometimes, if the second camera operation is not properly scrutinized, it can actually cost you time and money.

In THE CONVERSATION, Coppola and the production department agreed to use a second camera for the first two weeks. As you can tell from reading the script, many of the scenes which appear later in the story are actually different angles of scenes which appear earlier in the story. Having two cameras run simultaneously saved enormous amounts of time which would have been wasted had they needed to wait for the crew to move the camera to another SET-UP.

A Second Unit can be helpful. A true Second Unit has its own SECOND UNIT DIRECTOR, SECOND UNIT DIRECTOR OF PHOTOGRAPHY, and other key department heads. The production can break away some of their key members from First Unit and raise them to higher positions on Second Unit. For example, a SECOND ASSISTANT DIRECTOR on First Unit could be the First A.D. on Second Unit. Much depends on how independent the Second Unit is from the First Unit. In the case of *THE CONVERSATION* it was decided to keep the second camera as close to the First Unit as possible, and not let them actually break off and become a Second Unit.

In scripts which contain a lot of action and/or large crowd scenes, it is good to schedule additional cameras. But why be concerned here with additional cameras? You are going to need to know that the schedule you lay out is workable, that the amount of work (# of pages) you say can be shot in a day can actually be shot in a day. A second camera can aid in completing the day's (or night's) work. Each individual script together with the preferences of the director within the parameters of the budget will determine whether or not additional cameras are used.

12) **Special Equipment:** Wolfgang Glattes (co-producer STAR '80) was at one time involved with the film THE BOAT (*DAS BOOT*). When he was preparing his schedule, the availability of the German submarine was as important as the availability of any other parameter factor. In effect, the boat itself was considered to be a Cast Member.

You may find that you are going to need a SPECIAL PORTABLE CAMERA (e.g., Steadicam or Panaglide), and therefore, a SPECIAL CAMERA OPERATOR. Both the camera and the operator have to be scheduled as they are not always available and are quite costly. (Sometimes you will find that your camera operator is capable of operating the special camera, so you will only have to worry about the availability of the camera, not the operator.) A similar example can be made with **HELICOPTER SHOTS**. Not only do you need to rent a helicopter with a special camera mount, but also to hire a **HELICOPTER PILOT** who has flown helicopters to shoot films before and a **HELICOPTER CAMERA OPERATOR**.

13) **Geography of Location:** Sometimes the geography of the location can dictate the schedule lay-out. If the locations are spread all over the place, then hopefully the key locations will take precedence and it will be necessary to find alternate **SECONDARY LOCATIONS** closer to the **PRIMARY LOCATIONS**. For example, Harry's Warehouse (if actually shot on location) is a primary location whereas Amy's Apartment is a secondary location. If a suitable location is found for Harry's Warehouse but it is very far from Amy's Apartment location, unless there is a very good reason for not finding an alternate, a back-up location will be found for Amy's Apartment.

14) **Miscellaneous Factors:** You will come across other elements and factors which will affect the planning of your project. Always allow for the unexpected—your individual project will determine that.

# VII

## ARRANGING THE BOARD

Now that you understand the Parameter Factors, the first step in organizing your board will be to line up all your strips by location. Put all of the Union Square strips together in one space, all of Harry's Warehouse together, etc. Within each location, separate out the DAY and NIGHT material and put them together. Keep the strips in chronological order wherever possible. Use some of the black strips as dividers.

Don't by-pass this step and go on to the next step. This is a very important part of creating your production board.

Take the time now and arrange your board by locations. Please refer to the example in this chapter if you are unsure.

Once you have arranged the strips by location, you can now begin arranging them by cast within the various locations. By running your finger horizontally along the strips, you will see where each actor PLAYS (appears). Look for patterns. The first that you will see is that Stanley and Paul usually appear together, as do Mark and Ann. The only time all four actors appear together is in the UNION SQUARE sequence. Remembering that once you start an actor there must be enough drop-and-pick-up days in-between, you can see what would happen if you started your show with Union Square—either Ann and Mark or Stanley and Paul are going to do a lot of waiting around to complete their parts. As a result, you might be forced to return to a location later in the schedule to complete the actor's work. Such a DOUBLE-MOVE should be avoided. Also, it is better not to start the schedule with such a complicated scene. Give everyone time to get to know each other and work the bugs out before starting this.

As you can see, there are several scenes in which Harry works either alone or with characters who are in only one or two relatively small scenes, e.g., McNaught (the attorney), Harry's neighbors at *Harry's Apartment,* Amy at *Amy's Apartment,* etc. These scenes can be moved around the schedule with more flexibility than extremely complicated scenes or scenes involving other major characters.

Judging from the material in the script and the complexity of the plot, this is going to be an interesting screenplay to schedule. Go through your board and start grouping together the scenes which involve Harry alone, Harry with a minor character, Harry with Ann and/or Mark, Harry with Stanley and/or Paul. Just to keep things fairly straight here, group all Harry-alone scenes in the front of the board, and all Harry with minor-character scenes at the end of the board. In the middle put Harry with Ann/Mark, Harry with Ann/Mark/Stanley/Paul etc., and then Harry with Stanley/Paul. Put all miscellaneous scenes, especially the ones in which Harry doesn't appear at the end of the board, or in with the other scenes at the same location. Use your black strips to separate the locations. You may find that you are working with both ends of the board at the same time, going towards the middle.

Keep arranging and refining your board according to the Parameter Factors until you think that you have arrived at the best possible order. Don't start separating your board into days yet. One big question will loom up rather quickly—when to shoot the Union Square sequence? As you know from reading the screenplay several times, this is a key sequence. Should we do it right off and get it out of the way? We made the decision to schedule the Union Square sequence before the Warehouse sequence. Why? If you re-read the Warehouse sequence, you will see that Harry is going to play tapes of THE CONVERSA-TION in the warehouse. In order for him to actually play those tapes, they are going to have to be **PRE-RECORDED**. It is possi-ble that they could be pre-recorded in pre-production, or even dubbed in afterwards. However, in order to approach reality more closely, Mr. Coppola decided to record all the necessary dialogue on location so that not only would the actor's dialogue be recorded, so would all the requisite background noise. Therefore, we know that Ann and Mark's scenes in Union Square are going to have to be shot first so that there will be time enough to have the tapes and the still photographs of Ann and Mark by the time the warehouse is scheduled. Taking into consideration that the weather will be growing considerably worse as December approaches and that the Director needs a Christmas look, the Union Square sequence will have to be scheduled fairly early.

Now, keeping this in mind, see if you can roughly lay out your board. If you get stuck, refer to the Production Board fold-out.

**Title:** THE CONVERSATION
**Director:** FRANCIS COPPOLA
**Producer:**
**Asst. Director:**
**PROD'N MGR CLARK PAYLOW**

| | | | N | N | D | D | D | D | D | D | N | N | N | N | D | N | D | N |
|---|---|---|---|---|---|---|---|---|---|---|---|---|---|---|---|---|---|---|
| BREAKDOWN PAGE # | | | 46 | 47 | 104 | 105 | 106 | 108 | 40 | 41 | 42 | 43 | 44 | 48 | 49 | 377 | 380-397 | 378-379 |
| EXTERIOR OR INTERIOR | | | I | I | E | I | I | I | I | I | I | I | I | E | I | I | I | |
| SCENE # | | | 46 | 47 | 104 | 105 | 106 | 108 | 40 | 41 | 42 | 43 | 44 | 48 | 49 | 377 | 380-397 | 379 |
| Location | | | AMY'S BLDG.-HALL-APT. | AMY'S APT. | AMY'S APT. BLDG | AMY'S BLDG-HALL | AMY'S APT. | AMY'S APT. | HARRY'S APT. BLDG.-FOYER | HARRY'S APARTMENT | HARRY'S APT.-KITCHENETTE | HARRY'S APT. BLDG-Floor Hall | HARRY'S APT. | HARRY'S APT. | HARRY'S APT BLDG. | HARRY'S APT. BLDG | HARRY'S APARTMENT | HARRY'S APARTMENT |
| NO. OF PAGES | | | 2/8 | 5/8 | 1/8 | 2/8 | 1 3/8 | 1/8 | 3/8 | 1 | 1 7/8 | 3/8 | 3 5/8 | 3/8 | 1/8 | 4/8 | 2 7/8 | 3 |
| **Character** | **Artist** | **No.** | | | | | | | | | | | | | | | | |
| HARRY CAUL | | 1 | / | / | / | / | / | / | / | / | / | / | / | / | / | / | / | / |
| ANN | | 2 | | | | 2 V.O. | 2 V.O. | | | | | | | | | | | |
| MARK | | 3 | | | | | 3 V.O. | | | | | | | | | | | 3 V.O. |
| MR. C. | | 4 | | | | | | | | | | | | | | | | |
| STANLEY | | 5 | | | | | | | | | | | | | | | | |
| PAUL MEYERS | | 6 | | | | | | | | | | | | | | | | |
| MARTIN | | 7 | | | | | | | | | | | | | | | | |
| WILLIAM P. MORAN | | 8 | | | | | | | | | | | | | | | | |
| MEREDITH | | 9 | | | | | | | | | | | | | | | | |
| MILLARD | | 10 | | | | | | | | | | | | | | | | |
| MRS. GOETNER | | 11 | | | | | | | 11 | | 11 | | | | | | | |
| RON KELLER | | 12 | | | | | | | | | 12 | 12 | 12 | | | | | 12 |
| MRS. CORSITTO | | 13 | | | | | | | | | 13 | | 13 | | | | | |
| BOB | | 14 | | | | | | | | | 14 | 14 | 14 | | | | | 14 |
| BOB'S WIFE | | 15 | 16 V.O. | 16 | | | | | | | 15 | 15 | 15 | | | | | |
| AMY | | 16 | | | | | | | | | | | | | | | | |
| LURLEEN | | 17 | | | | | | | | | | | | | | | | |
| MALE SEC'Y | TONY | 18 / 19 | | | | | | | | | | | | | | | | 18 V.O. |
| MALE RECEPT. | MIME | 20 / 21 | | | | | | | | | | | | | | | | |
| YOUNG MAN | YOUNG WOMAN | 22 / 23 | | | | | | | | | | | | | | | | |
| SHOPPER #1 | SHOPPER #2 | 24 / 25 | | | | | | | | | | | | | | | | |
| SHOPPER #3 | LAUNDRY LADY | 26 / 27 | | | | | | | | | | | | | | | | |
| #27'S LITTLE BOY | WOMAN #1-ELEV | 28 / 29 | | | | | | | | | | | | | | | | |
| WOMAN #2-ELEV | MAN IN ELEVATOR | 30 / 31 | | | | | | | | | | | | | | | | |
| DEMO MAN | SPEAKER | 32 / 33 | | | | | | | | | | | | | | | | |
| MAN IN BOOTH | YOUNG DRIVER | 34 / 35 | | | | | | | | | | | | | | | | |
| MOTEL CLERK | BUS DRIVER #1 | 36 / 37 | | | | | | | | | | | | | | | | |
| BUS DRIVER #2 | MCNAUGHT | 38 / 39 | | | | | | | | | | | | | | | | |
| ANNC'R/PA SYS. | TEL. OPER. #1 | 40 / 41 | | | | | | | | | | | | | | | | |
| CHROME DOME VO. | WOMAN IN ROOM | 42 / 43 | | | | | | | | | | | | | | | | |
| TEL. OPER. #2 | MAN #2 IN BOOTH | 44 / 45 | | | | | | | | | | | | | | | | |

MUSIC: (M)   CARS: (C)
SPECIAL EQUIPMENT: (SE)
ANIMALS: (A)
EXTRAS: (#)

- 46: CLIMBS STAIRS, ENTERS APT
- 47: HARRY VISITS AMY
- 104: ENTERS BLDG
- 105: OPENS AMY'S DOOR
- 106: AMY'S GONE
- 108: STAND IN EMPTY APT.
- 40: CHECKS MAIL, GREETS NEIGHBOR
- 41: HARRY CALLS APT. MANAGER
- 42: DISTURBED BY TENANTS
- 43: BOB TALKS TO HARRY
- 44: BIRTHDAY PARTY
- 48: HARRY PLAYS SAX
- 49: HARRY EXITS BUILDING
- 377: PASSES RON ON STAIRCASE
- 380-397: SEARCHES FOR WIRETAP  * THE END *
- 378-379: TRIES MR. C'S OFFICE, CONFRONTS NEIGHBORS

| | | | | | | | | | | | | | | | | | | | | | | | | |
|---|---|---|---|---|---|---|---|---|---|---|---|---|---|---|---|---|---|---|---|---|---|---|---|---|
| D | D | | D | D | D | D | D | D | D | D | D | D | N | N | N | N | N | N | N | N | N | N | N | D |
| 93-94 | 95 | | 50 | 51-57 | 59-61 | 63 | 65 | 67 | 69-70 | 72-80 | 82-86 | 88-91 | 160 | 161-173 | 174-181 | 183-184 | 186-187 | 333-336 | 337-339 | 340-353 | 355 | 357-358 | 362 | 364 | 230 |
| I | I | | E | I | I | I | I | I | I | I | I | I | I | I | I | I | I | E | I | I | I | I | I | I | I |
| 93-94 | 95 | | 50 | 51-57 | 59-61 | 63 | 65 | 67 | 69-70 | 72-80 | 82-86 | 88-91 | 160 | 161-173 | 174-181 | 183-184 | 186-187 | 333-336 | 337-339 | 340-353 | 355 | 357-358 | 362 | 364 | 230 |
| LAWYER'S OFFICE | LAWYER'S OFF. & STUDY | | HARRY'S WARE HOUSE | H'S WAREHOUSE WORK AREA | H'S WARE HOUSE WORK AREA | H'S WAREHOUSE WORK AREA | H'S WARE HOUSE WORK AREA | H'S WARE HOUSE WORK AREA | H'S WARE HOUSE WORK AREA | H'S WARE HOUSE WORK AREA | H'S WARE HOUSE WORK AREA | H'S WARE HOUSE WORK AREA | H'S WARE HOUSE WORK AREA | H'S WARE HOUSE WORK AREA | H'S WARE HOUSE WORK AREA | H'S WARE HOUSE WORK AREA | H'S WARE HOUSE WORK AREA | H'S WARE HOUSE – ALLEY | H'S WARE HOUSE – STAIRCASE | HARRY'S WARE HOUSE | H'S WARE HOUSE – WORK AREA | H'S WARE HOUSE – WORK AREA | H'S WARE HOUSE – WORK AREA | H'S WARE HOUSE – WORK AREA | CATHOLIC CHURCH |
| 2 3/8 | 2 7/8 | | 2 3/8 | 2 4/8 | 3/8 | 1/8 | 3/8 | 3/8 | 7/8 | 1 3/8 | 1 | 4/8 | 1/8 | 19 7/8 | 9 7/8 | 2/8 | 5/8 | 4/8 | 3/8 | 3 7/8 | 2/8 | 3/8 | 1/8 | 1/8 | 2/8 |
| REVEALED AS OWNER/SEES TONY | TONY CRIES. TELLS STORY | | ENTERS HIS WARE HOUSE | DISCUSS CONVENTION/WORK | C.J. EQUIP./HARRY | LISTENS TO CONVERSATION | PLAYS IT AGAIN | HARRY-STANLEY DISAGREE | WORKS ON FILTERING CONVERSATION | WORKS ON CONVERSATION | WORKS ON CONVERSATION | WORKS ON CONVERSATION | EST. SHOT–WORK AREA | THEY PARTY, LEAVE | THEY LISTEN, SLEEP | REEL TURNS, HARRY SLEEPS | AWAKENS–MEREDITH'S GONE | DISCOVERS BREAK IN | CLIMBS STAIRS | CHASES INTRUDER AWAY | HARRY LISTENS, REMEMBERS | STARES AT PLAYING TAPE | LISTENS TO TAPE | TURNS OFF RECORDER | GOES TO CONFESSION |

# VIII

## HOW MANY DAYS?

Now that you have arranged your board according to the Parameter Factors, you can start to determine the amount of time it is going to take to film each location.

Until now, most of the work was manual—lining the script, filling in the breakdown sheets and preparing the strips. Now comes the hard part—determining how much time everything is going to need. Unfortunately, there is no real formula and your ability to guess correctly will improve with experience.

If the director has not been hired, ask the producers whom they have in mind and then do some research. Find out what the director (or director-candidate) has done in the past and speak to those in production (production manager). To find out what a director's most recent credits are, either look in *FILM DIRECTORS: A Complete Guide (Lone Eagle Publishing)* or call the Directors Guild of America (if the director is a member of the DGA). You will probably need to call the production companies to find out who the production manager and/or assistant directors were on the show. Ask the production manager and/or the A.D. how the director organizes his work. *Does he stay on schedule? Has the director done this kind of material before? Does the director work well with actors? What about action scenes?* If you are blessed, you will be fortunate to be working with a director who does both well—actors and action. Ask more questions—*How long a day does the director like to work?* Some directors, like Sidney Lumet, are well organized and like to go home at a reasonable time. These are but a few questions you should ask those who have experienced the director before. Always remember that you must weigh the director's past work. A key rule: The director always sets the pace on the set.

Next, you should ask the producer and director (if hired) whom they have in mind as DIRECTOR OF PHOTOGRAPHY. The DP (called DOP in England and Australia) is a key person and his methods of shooting can and do play a major role in determining how much time it is going to take to shoot each scene. There are DP's who take a great deal of time to light a set (the term "location" is interchangeable here), and then there are others, especially those who have a strong television background who move quickly through the scripted material. If you can find out who is being considered, then you will be able to create a more workable, realistic schedule.

We are scheduling a five-day work week (Monday through Friday) because THE CONVERSATION is considered an IN-TOWN show, and not a LOCATION PICTURE which uses a six-day (Monday through Saturday) schedule. This will make more of a difference in budgeting then in scheduling.

Start with scenes involving only Harry (if possible). Try to give the actor and the director some working time together. Stay away from scenes which involve heavy preparation (action, special effects, make-up, stunts, large numbers of principal actors, crowd scenes, intimate or highly emotional scenes, etc.) Since principal photography has been scheduled for late November, just after Thanksgiving, it would be wise to do as many exteriors as possible. In January, the weather (even in San Francisco) isn't the best. Although you can plan your schedule for any time period during the year, we thought it would be more interesting to schedule this show over the same time period that it was actually shot.

In looking over the board and taking all the Parameters into consideration, here, then is the schedule which we feel works best.

## DAY 1 -
### Sunday, November 26

EXT. - Financial District - DAY (195 - 198) 5/8
EXT. - Financial District Phone Booth - DAY (226 - 229) 4/8
EXT. - Golden Gate Park - DAY (188 - 194) 2-3/8
Total - 3-4/8 pages

The first day of the schedule and we have already broken a rule: we're starting on Sunday, not Monday. You have a location— the Financial District—which has to look two ways: active and desolate. Short of stopping all traffic and business in that area to shoot the necessary scenes during the week, the only way to accomplish this is to shoot it on a weekend when offices are closed and the streets will be empty. Since you are going to have your crew available and working on Sunday, and you are going to have to pay them the minimum call, it makes sense to sched- ule more than just one little 1/8 of a page scene. Refer to your script, when Harry walks into the Financial District building and into the empty elevator area (Scene 198). This scene would also be difficult to stage on a normally busy day. After Harry's meeting upstairs with Mr. C., we see him walking through a bleak and desolate financial district (Scenes 226 - 229). He stops and makes a phone call. In the script, you will find an earlier scene in which Harry confronts Stanley. He does this in Scenes 188 - 194 in Golden Gate Park—on a Sunday. This is more of a coincidence than a deciding factor, but it gives you another scene which can be shot that same day. Ok, now, *which* Sunday. If you begin on a Sunday, then you will avoid the TURN-AROUND problem which would face you if you tried to shoot this after having worked on the previous Friday. So, let's schedule it first and get it over with. Remember that you are going to have to give your actors a certain number of hours off before they can work again. If you do not do this, you will find yourself in a FORCED CALL situation—not giving them enough time off—and having to pay dearly for it.

If you tried to shoot this Sunday sequence later on in the schedule, you would be severely limiting the material you could shoot in the latter part of the week before. Keeping possible weather problems in mind, it makes sense to get this over with first.

As we stated—shooting on a Sunday is an exception, not a rule. If you are looking for an average, or more normal way to start a shooting schedule, then begin on a Wednesday. It gives the director and crew a couple of days to get used to each other, renew old acquaintances etc., and then two days off before you get into full swing. It also gives the cast and crew the time during the early part of the week to make any last minute necessary changes before DAY ONE.

The page count for the day is an ambitious 3-4/8 pages.

### DAY 2
**Monday, November 27.**

EXT. Electric Bus/Neighborhood - DAY (34, 36, 37) - 3/8
INT. Electric Bus - DAY (35) - 2/8

INT. Market - DAY (38) - 1/8
Total - 6/8 pages.

It is Monday. We are going to do more exterior work with Harry alone. In order to film the inside of the market, it will probably be necessary for the crew to go in and PRE-LIGHT (take out the flourescent light bulbs and replace them with color-corrected bulbs, hang additional lights, etc.) and PRE-RIG (put up any scaffolding, ceiling mounts for the lights). Part of the crew can be working on this while the other part of the crew is working on the Exteriors and the Interior of the Bus. Although 6/8 of a page doesn't seem like very much, laying out street action and coordinating it is not an easy task, especially considering the light availability problem at this time of the year. This will be a busy second day's work.

## DAY 3
### Tuesday, November 28

EXT. Street - Burning Car - DAY (365) 1/8
EXT. Electric Bus - NIGHT (45) 1/8
Total - 2/8 pages.

Mr. C. (*Robert Duvall*) works in three distinctly different locations—his office, the motel room and the burning Mercedes Benz. Your question to the director should be, "Does the person in the burning car have to be the actor or can it be a STUNT PHOTO DOUBLE?" (a stunt person who closely resembles the actor). If a photo double can be used, then you have more flexibility in scheduling the time to shoot this scene. In this case, both the producer and the director wanted Duvall to be in the scene and not doubled. Until now, we have not STARTED any other key actor except for Stanley. Based upon the special effects requirements and control which will be mandatory by the Police and Fire Departments, and since this is a Day Exterior, it would be advisable to do this scene as early as possible in the schedule. Mr. C may be your first drop-and-pick-up. Keep that in mind as you schedule his next work—making sure that you keep at least ten calendar days between his last day of work and the next day of work. Most likely, Ann and Mark will have started working and you will be able to schedule one of Mr. C.'s two remaining scenes then.

The burning car scene will have to be shot in a remote area approved by the local authorities. This forces the film crew to pack up and move after completing the scene. Because of the loss of time and resulting loss of light, it makes sense to schedule a Night Exterior. Keep in mind that it must be a simple one in order to finish early. If we film late into the night, we will face a possible turn-around problem the next day. Since we were filming the Electric Bus sequence the day before and the cast, crew, director, etc., are all familiar with it, why not schedule it for this day and get Scene 45 - Exterior Electric Bus - Night, out of the way? It only involves Harry and has a value of 1/8 of a page.

## DAY 4
### Wednesday, November 29

EXT. Financial District - DAY (96, 97) 2/8
EXT. Financial Plaza - DAY (271, 272) 2/8
EXT. Director's Bldg. - DAY (282, 283) 3/8
Total - 7/8 pages

With the aim of finishing our Day Exteriors as early into the schedule as possible, we return to a location: Financial District, Plaza - Director's Building. Here we are barely four days into a schedule and we have already broken two rules which we gave you. The first, we started our schedule on a Sunday and now we are returning to a location. If you look at the scenes for this

76

location you will see that we need two completely different looks—one busy and one desolate. As we mentioned before, it would take a lot of work and probably cost more money to try to shoot both of these looks at the same time. Therefore, it makes more sense to return.

In Scenes 96 and 97, Harry walks across the busy street, through the plaza towards the escalator. In Scene 271, Harry moves quickly through the crowded Financial Plaza. In 272, we see Harry's POV of the Director's building in the Plaza. In Scene 282, Ann walks out of the Director's building and down the street. Harry follows her. In Scene 283, Ann walks toward and boards an Electric Bus. Harry follows and boards the bus behind. Scenes 96, 97, 271, 272, 282 and 283 all require a crowded plaza. Therefore, we have scheduled these scenes together. In Scene 283, the script calls for "low fog". This would be noted on your breakdown sheets and would be a question you would ask your director.

## DAYS 5,6
### Thursday, November 30; Friday, December 1

EXT. Union Square - DAY.
(1-9, 58, 62, 64, 66, 68, 71, 87, 107) - 6-7/8.
Total - 6-7/8 pages

The key sequence for this film is UNION SQUARE where "the conversation" takes place. It is all exterior day work. Scenes and voice-overs of Ann and Mark's conversation at this location are used throughout the remainder of the screenplay. At first glance, you may think that Scenes 62, 64 etc., are merely repeats of Scene 9. On further inspection and analysis, however, we see the subtle difference which make this script so fascinating, and so complicated to do. Be careful. Don't automatically call a scene a repeat unless it is *exactly* the same.

As mentioned earlier, when at all possible, it is best to shoot all scenes at a certain location in sequential order. It works to the director's and actors' advantage—allowing them to build a performance. It is also quite helpful in MATCHING.

We shall continue using a second camera to get the necessary COVERAGE for the work we have scheduled. Alfred Hitchcock once said that a motion picture is merely a series of still photographs. This sequence in Union Square is an excellent illustration. Through proper and thorough coverage, a series of scenes works throughout the entire film. It should be noted that coverage of a scene should be laid out intelligently. Excessive shooting of angles which are not used in the completed editing are a waste of time and money.

In THE CONVERSATION, Mr. Coppola has given the reader just enough information to form an opinion. As the story progresses, we learn more and more through Harry and find out that what we thought we heard—that the "poor young couple. Ann and Mark," who are deeply in love and are in danger of being found out—is not really true at all. Actually the "poor young couple" is using Harry Caul in their plot to murder Ann's husband, Mr. C. Through Harry, they force Mr. C. into a neutral, unguarded location where they can , and do, murder him. As the story progresses, we finally figure this all out and realize that Harry has been used. How did Mr. Coppola do this? The board tells us all the scripted scene numbers for the Union Square sequence. Let's go deeper and analyze the surveillance of "the conversation" and see how that "conversation" was written. We shall begin with Scene 1.

**Scene 1**
We begin with a MEDIUM SHOT (View) of EXT. Union Square. A small band of street musicians have just set up in the park.

**Scene 2**
HIGH FULL SHOT (wide) establishing the downtown area of
San Francisco. The Union Square is in the center of the frame.
From the script we know that it is lunchtime on a workday
sometime close to Christmas. Both are established in this shot
through wardrobe, set dressing and props.

**Scene 3**
Here Coppola planned to begin his MAIN TITLES. The camera
begins to ZOOM in on the park at Union Square. The shot ends
on the Young Mime who is imitating certain passers-by walking
down a walkway.

**Scene 4**
The camera goes to a close shot (view) of the musicians we saw
in Scene 1. One musician puts down his instrument and begins
to tap dance.

**Scene 5**
The camera draws in to a close shot (view) of the tapping shoes.

**Scene 6**
A shot of the mime imitating a middle-aged man who is OFF-
CAMERA.

**Scene 7**
The director shows us who the mime is imitating, and intro-
duces HARRY CAUL—the main character of the film.

**Scene 8**
The camera cuts back to the musicians. The saxophonist is
playing a solo. The crowd, including Harry, is delighted. The
musicians play, "Red, Red Robin."

**Scene 9**

Two other lead characters are introduced—ANN and MARK. We see them pass Harry and join the spectators watching the band. They make a few comments. Ann sings along a few lines of "Red, Red Robin." They walk away, leaving Harry. They come upon an old derelict asleep on a park bench. Ann is upset. They talk about the derelict and then move on. They pass Harry again, talking. This time, however, the sound is coming from off-screen. As Ann and Mark pass, Harry gets up off the bench where he is sitting and walks toward a small panel van truck. The camera moves up the face of the building to the roof where we see a man holding a shotgun microphone. We hear what he is listening to—Ann and Mark's conversation.

From this point, we would not go on to Scene 10 because it would require a major camera move to the roof of the building to see the scene from his point of view. What about having a second camera on the roof? Well, the only problem would be that if you shot Scene 9 in one continuous take and there were a camera on the roof, you would run into the possibility of seeing the camera in the end of the shot.

As you will see when you look at the Shooting Schedule in Chapter IX, the work for Days 5 & 6 has been divided into two sections—Scenes 1-9 and the rest of the scenes. Notice also that Harry is not listed on the schedule for the scenes after 1-9. In reading the script closely, you will see that Harry is not really needed. The mention of him in Scene 58 is actually a repeat of scene 9. Since Harry Caul is a run-of-show player, the director felt that it would be best to give him a few days off. He is not needed again until Day 10.

**Scene 58**

This scene is intercut into the Warehouse sequence where Harry studies the tapes. This scene will appear in the film, but notice that Ann and Mark's dialogue appears to be coming off-screen. This tells us that the dialogue we are hearing for this part of Scene 9 was recorded from somewhere else so as to give a feeling of surveillance.

## Scene 62
Again, we find Ann and Mark repeating lines which we heard in Scene 9, but this time there is a difference. Here as Harry works on making a better recording, he brings out dialogue which we haven't heard before. This is new information which actually expands what we heard and saw in Scene 9.

## Scene 64
In Scene 9, Ann and Mark walk up to an old derelict. This is a piece of coverage of that scene which is not used until now in the chronology of the film.

## Scene 66
In Scene 9, Ann and Mark walk past the derelict. Additional dialogue is introduced. This is a new scene and again, part of the coverage of Scene 9 but used later in the script and noted with a new scene number. Again, Harry is building "the conversation" through the use of electronics.

## Scene 68
Here, we have two lines, *MARK: "Where'd you hear that?"* in *Scene 18* and, *MARK: "It's a nice day today; yesterday it was cold and foggy,"* - Scene 22. Scene 18 as you see is a scene to be shot from the roof of the building. Scene 22 is of Paul following Ann and Mark. Scene 68 does not include Paul. We see the Mime in the background imitating Ann and Mark. As you see in Scene 19, which we are also not doing now, the Mime does his imitation to the crowd's amusement. Scene 68 actually gives us coverage of the surveillance from Scene 17 where we get some dialogue to the middle of Scene 22. This additional

coverage leads us through Harry's eventual discovery of Ann and Mark's plot.

### Scene 71
This is a close shot of Ann which widens to include Mark. Paul passes by in the shot. This is actually coverage of the end of Scene 22, "An expression of fear comes to her (Ann's) face", and Scene 24 (telescopic view from the roof of the building.) Ann remarks to Mark about the man with the hearing aid and Mark tries to comfort her.

### Scene 87
This is additional dialogue for Scene 27. *MARK: "You go . . ."* *ANN: "You really don't, but I want to kiss you."* This scene is on Ann and Mark and part of the dialogue is used as off-screen lines inside the Panel Van Truck.

### Scene 107
This scene is actually the last part of Scene 87. This could be a separate SET-UP from Scene 87 of Ann leaning forward and giving Mark a kiss as she is about to deliver her line.

All these scenes keep us at ground level on the Square. It is obvious that it will take more than one day, but it should not take more than two. How does one arrive at that conclusion. Well, let's look at the factors. We have six pages of material to do. There are four principal actors involved and, with the exception of contracting the Square for SET-UPS (Camera moves), the dialogue should not take more than two days.

You have now completed Week One. You will continue working on the Union Square material on Monday, since you have probably run out of light now after having completed six pages.

## DAY 7
## Monday, December 4

EXT. Union Square - DAY (Scene 19-22, 81, 28, 33, 182, 185, 222) 2-4/8
Total - 2-4/8 pages.

It's Monday morning and we are back in Union Square. As we said before, you should continue with a location lowest scene number first.

### Scene 19
We're staying at ground level so the first scene is 19. The Mime does a burlesque of Ann and Mark

### Scenes 20, 21 and 22
The sequence continues in Scene 20, a MOVING VIEW of Ann and Mark who do not see the Mime's imitation of them. We introduce Paul in Scene 21. This leads us to Scene 22 where we see Paul trying to stay close to Ann and Mark in order to pick up their conversation. This part of the ground level sequence ends when Ann notices Paul. He realizes that he has been pointed out and passes by, hoping to avoid further interest. The sequence shifts to a shot from high up in an open window which will be done, once we complete all the ground level material. We did not try to schedule this material on Friday because we probably would have run out of light and the scenes wouldn't have matched.

### Scene 81
Time to break another rule again "Try to shoot in sequence at a location." Chronologically, Scene 81 should be shot later on. However, as we can read from the script, Scene 81 is actually

coverage of Scene 26 (telescopic view from the roof of the building) but with additional dialogue. Ann and Mark are walking by the bongo drum players. Here we pick up the line, ". . . *kill us.*", from Mark. So, in terms of scene numbers, we are shooting out of sequence, but in terms of material, we are in sequence—just a different angle of the same scene.

### Scene 28
Here we see Ann and Mark part. The surveillance is over.

### Scene 33
The street band of musicians put away their instruments. Lunch time is about over and they collect the tips which have been put into the top hat.

### Scene 182
This is another angle of the conversation between Ann and Mark. In this walking scene in the square, we can see the anxiety and fear underlining their expressions. This shot could have been done anytime during a scene involving them from Scene 9, where they meet, to Scene 28, where they part.

### Scene 185
Again, as we saw in Scene 182, we can hear no dialogue but see that Ann and Mark are talking. This scene could be done anytime the camera is on them from Scene 9 to Scene 28.

### Scene 222
Here we find Ann and Mark walking along. They comment on Paul. By checking the script, we find that this is actually 3/4's of Scene 24. But Scene 24 is to be shot from high up giving us a telescopic view. This scene is ground level on Ann and Mark and is shot from a different camera position.

This day we covered 2-4/8 pages. Dealing with the crowd control problem in the square and the staging of these scenes, you have a good, hard Monday scheduled.

## DAYS 8 & 9
### Tuesday, December 5; Wednesday, December 6

EXT. - Union Square - Eiffel Tower - DAY
EXT. - Office Building Windows - DAY
(10, 11, 25, 26, 17, 31, 18, 23, 24, 103, 32, 13, 30) - 3-2/8
Total - 3-2/8 pages.

**Scene 10**
Beginning with the lowest scene number first, we find ourselves on the roof of the Eiffel Tower Sign Building. We are looking at Union Square from the POV (Point of View) of the Man On Roof With The Shotgun Microphone, at the people in the Square.

**Scene 11**
A close-up of Ann talking with Mark.

**Scene 25**
Man On Roof With Shotgun Microphone scans the people in the square through the telescopic sights on his microphone. He looks for Ann and Mark. (**Note:** Any of the "effects" of looking through a telescopic lens - i.e., cross-hairs, will be added later on. That is an OPTICAL EFFECT which is added in the laboratory.)

**Scene 26**
Continuation of the Man's POV as he watches Ann and Mark walk past the bongo players. This is another angle of Scene 81

which we scheduled for Day 7 where Mark says the words, *". . . kill us."* In this scene (26), we hear Mark's opening of that line, *"He'd . . . chance"* the rest of which is obliterated by the sound of the bongo drums.

### Scene 17
We pan from the man under the Eiffel Tower sign to another man in an office building window.

### Scene 31
The surveillance is over. The Man begins to disassemble his shotgun microphone.

This finishes the rooftop sequence. We now move to the Office Building Window where Another Man is tracking Ann and Mark's movements.

### Scene 18
This is a POV shot of Ann and Mark and is actually coverage of Scene 68 which we scheduled for Day 5 or 6.

### Scene 23
The Man In The Open Window adjusts his microphone sights.

### Scene 24
This is a shot of Ann and Mark from the Man In The Open Window's POV. The shot opens with a Close-Up of Ann's face to a TWO-SHOT. Ann comments on seeing Paul. Mark tries to dispell her fears—does all this dialogue sound familiar? This is actually the MASTER SHOT of Scene 71 done from a high angle. In actuality, Scene 71 is Coverage of this scene. Why then, is this the Master Shot? Because, the information which is given in Scene 24 is actually greater than the information in Scene 71 and, on closer inspection, you will also see that Scene 71 is actually only 3/4's of the length of Scene 24.

**Scene 103**
This is a repeat of part of Scene 24.

**Scene 32**
The surveillance is over. The Man In The Open Window disassembles his equipment.

Now that all the scenes from the top of the buildings are completed, we shall move back down to the ground and finish the scenes which we have left to do there. Why didn't we schedule this ground work when we were on the ground before? For one reason, many of these shots are close and you wouldn't see all the extras which were needed for the wide shots and high-angle shots of Union Square. Also, since most of the action occurs around the van, we could always have used this as a Cover Set —something which could be shot easily if need be. This is an easily controllable sequence. We shall try to finish the exteriors first.

**Scene 13**
In this scene, the two Secretaries pass in front of the mirrored panel van and fix their make-up. From the script, we know that Stanley is inside, making comments. Keep in mind that whatever action the secretaries do will have to be repeated on a separate day for the Interior shots, otherwise, the action won't match. We say a separate day, as by now we will probably be running out of light and, therefore, time. If possible, we should try to get this shot quickly and then Scene 30 before we run out of light.

**Scene 30**
This a simple ESTABLISHING SHOT of the van sitting at the curb. It would be a good idea to have the Second Camera which has been with you doing additional coverage of the scenes set

up their camera for this shot so that as soon as Scene 13 is done and the set is cleared, they can get this shot quickly.

## DAY 10
### Thursday, December 7

INT. - Paneled Van - DAY
(12, 14-16, 17, 29) 4-4/8
Total - 4-4/8 pages.

All the exterior filming for the Union Square sequence was scheduled first and now, after five days, we are ready to proceed with the Interior of the Paneled Van Truck. If this had been a regular van without any mirrors, we probably wouldn't have scheduled it here. It is essential to the plot, however that we see out the windows onto Union Square.

### Scene 12

Beginning with the lowest scene number scheduled for this location, we bring Stanley back to work. He worked on DAY 1 in the park. We have carried him for 8 days (paid him). After today, we will drop him and pick him up later. He is going to be paid for 10 days work although he actually only worked 2. Unfair? Well, if it had been scheduled differently it might have cost a lot more. The importance of scheduling Union Square at this time of the year carries more of a priority than Stanley's Hold Days. If you refer back to your Parameter Factors you will see that Locations are the Number One parameter and Cast is Number Two.

Harry enters the van in this scene. We become aware of his involvement in the recording of Ann and Mark's conversation.

### Scenes 14, 15 & 16

Because of the cramped quarters of the Panel Van Truck, these three scenes will probably be shot back to back without really changing camera positions. We begin with a shot of the secretaries fixing their make-up in front of the mirrors. Then we watch Stanley egg them on in Scene 15, unbeknownst to the secretaries, and then in Scene 16, we discover more about Stanley, Harry and the conversation they are recording. We find out that the equipment they are using is sophisticated and that they are professionals.

## Scene 27
As Harry and Stanley continue their surveillance, Paul—dejected at having been discovered by Ann—enters the van, and drops off his recording and surveillance equipment. This scene appears to be simple, but there are actually three actors speaking in addition to Ann and Mark's off-screen lines. The writer/director also mentions seeing the afternoon traffic through the mirrors. This should probably be done as a separate shot or set-up. Because of the cramped conditions, the director may be forced to try for a Master Shot involving all three actors and then go to OVER-THE-SHOULDER SHOTS and Close-Ups on each to get his coverage. Confined quarters such as these severely limit movement.

## Scene 29
The surveillance is over. The couple has parted. Stanley opens the scene by re-winding the tape recorders. As we have seen in all the UNION SQUARE sequences up to now, there has been a definite "end of surveillance" sequence. The "end of surveillance" sequence begins here with Stanley professionally shutting the operation down while Harry makes a joke.

Judging from the scripted scenes, Ann and Mark really only work in the first scene (Scene 12). Once this scene has been completed, the director will probably allow these two actors to go home for the day. As you progress through the scenes in sequential order, you will find that the need to control the

Exterior (except for excess noise while recording inside the van) will diminish. You are going to cover 4-4/8ths pages today— ambitious but plausible.

This finishes the Union Square location. It took six days to do this work and you completed over 17 pages. Simple division tells you that you are doing almost 3 pages per day. Resist the temptation to generalize like this. Many times, especially in television where schedules are shorter by economic necessity, the production office and/or producer will try to come up with an average page count per day and have the director adhere to it. If you look over the last ten days, you will see that there have been days where we scheduled over 6 pages of work and other days where you were going to be lucky to complete 2/8 of a page. It depends on the material and the other factors needed to shoot the scene. Many times, the shooting of the scene is what takes the least amount of time. It's the getting there, setting up and then packing up that takes the time. You will learn to weigh material and come up with accurate (or more accurate) schedules the more you practice.

Also remember that if you have a first-time director who has not worked with actors before, chances are that it is going to take you longer to complete the work. The director in this instance, *Francis Coppola,* had directed six feature films prior to THE CONVERSATION. His knowledge of the script and his experience with actors were key factors in determining the amount of time each sequence would take to complete.

### DAY 11
### Friday, December 8

INT. - Amy's Apartment - NIGHT (46, 47) 5-5/8
Total - 5-5/8 pages.

The six days we just completed were all out of doors. Taking the time of year into consideration and the chance of inclement weather (which wouldn't match), it is always a good idea to have a cover set. The Panel Van Truck sequence was one, and this is another. A good cover set is one which can be switched to almost immediately. The Panel Van Truck sequence used the actors which we were already using—Harry, Stanley, Paul (and Ann and Mark). The sequence in Amy's Apartment needs only Harry and Amy. In addition to having the location pre-rigged and pre-lit, we must make arrangements for the actress playing Amy (Teri Garr) to be available not only on this day, but also on any of the other six days we are at Union Square. It is quite important to check the actor's, in this case actress' availability. If you need to call her in earlier than scheduled and have officially placed her on hold so that she cannot accept other employment, you will have to pay her for those days, worked or not.

A cover set such as this can also be used to help stretch the time necessary for a drop and pick-up. This sequence at Amy's apartment lasts for two days. If we found ourselves in a situation where we didn't have enough time between drop and pickups on Stanley, Mr. C., or possibly Ann and Mark, this sequence could be slotted into the schedule so that we would have the necessary 10 calendar days.

We begin this location with Scene 46—written as a Night scene. Not knowing what the actual location looks like, whether you can see from the inside that it is night, we have scheduled this location for Friday so that it could possibly be shot at night if need be. Generally, it is easier and less expensive to shoot most night interiors during the day and black out the windows.

In this scene, Harry comes to visit Amy, the girl he keeps. It is his birthday, and he walks in with the bottle of wine which

91

Mrs. Evangelista gave him. He walks up the staircase (Scene 46) and enters the room (Scene 47). If we had used it as a cover set and some of the scenes needed to be shot at night, we would have re-arranged the order in which they were shot to accommodate the location.

This sequence runs almost six pages. It is also dramatic material between two people. There are no stunts or special effects involved. Since Coppola likes to rehearse his actors before the actual production begins, we are confident that we will be able to finish this material in one day.

## DAY 12
### Monday, December 11

EXT. - Amy's Apartment - DAY (104) 1/8
INT. - Amy's Apartment Building - DAY (105) 2/8
INT. - Amy's Apartment Bedroom - DAY (106) 1-3/8
INT. - Amy's Apartment Bedroom - DAY (108) 1/8
Total - 1-7/8 pages

### Scene 104
It's Monday and we have returned to Amy's apartment. Beginning with the exterior work first. Amy worked in Friday's material. Today involves only Harry.

### Scene 105
We move inside to the hallway scene where we observe Harry has abandoned his usually cautious manner. He opens the door.

### Scenes 106 & 108
Harry finds that Amy has left him. Ann and Mark's conversation plays back in the background. Whether or not the director wants to use a playback of Ann and Mark's lines is a question

you will have to ask. In order to better control this scene and to place the emphasis on Harry's not finding Amy—and not on Ann and Mark's dialogue, we would suggest using a playback.

All of this dialogue is close to two pages. If things work as planned, this should be a fairly light day and you will complete the location today. You don't have to (and shouldn't try) to kill yourself and your crew every day. It might happen that you didn't finish all of last week's work and had to shoot some of Amy's material today. A light day gives you the opportunity to catch up.

## DAY 13
### Tuesday - December 12

INT. - Director's Building Elevator - DAY (98, 199, 276–281)
INT. - Dir. Bldg. - Lobby - Newsstand - DAY 366-368) 5/8
Total - 2-3/8 pages.

**Scene 98**
We go into the elevator of the Director's building. This time it is crowded with people as Harry heads for the penthouse.

**Scene 199**
Harry is inside the elevator. He is alone. It arrives at the lobby. Since it is supposed to be Sunday, you should make sure to keep the area around the elevator clear.

**Scenes 276 - 281**
All are taken inside the elevator. As with the Panel Van Truck scenes, shooting in an elevator is difficult and cramped. These five scenes are very short and involve no dialogue at all. While these scenes are being shot, the rest of the crew will be downstairs preparing for the next sequence of shots.

**Scenes 366 - 368**
Harry looks down at a stack of newspapers. Depending on what the director wants to show in the scene, Scene 367 could be shot as an INSERT—i.e., a shot which is done either earlier or later and inserted in the editing. Holding the important blue pouch in his arms, he walks off toward the elevators.

If we had done this group of shots first, we might have had some crowd control problems as we would have been shooting just as everyone was arriving for work in the elevator. Hopefully, by scheduling this later in the day, we can finish these scenes either before or after everyone who works in the building will need to get in the elevators to go home.

## DAY 14
### Wednesday, December 13

INT. - Lobby - Director's Office - DAY (200–205) 1 page
INT. - Reception - Director's Office - DAY (273–275) 1-1/8
INT. - Reception - Director's Office - DAY (369–376) 1 page
Total - 3-1/8 pages.

**Scenes 200-205**
Again, the look should be that of an office on Sunday—empty and quiet. The only thing that may cause any difficulty at all is the dog which is used in Scene 204. Other than that, this sequence should go smoothly. There is no dialogue and not a lot of action.

**Scenes 273-275**
Now we need to fill in with extras, as this is supposed to be taking place during the week. We introduce the Receptionist who doesn't want Harry to go back to the Director's office.

**Scenes 369–376**
Practically a repeat of 200 to 205, except that the reception area is crowded with people, including Ann and Mark.

As you can see, we have scheduled the scenes to be done in sequence in a controlled atmosphere. We have gone from the less difficult to the more difficult as we did the day before. In order to make the sequence work effectively, we are going to have to get coverage of Ann and Mark, as well as other actors in this sequence. We are planning to shoot more than three pages today. Until this last sequence, the day should move along very quickly. We will try to finish Scenes 200-205 and 273-275 before lunch so that the afternoon can be spent getting this sequence.

## DAY 15
### Thursday, December 14

INT. Director's Reception - DAY (Scene 99) 1-4/8
INT. Director's Corridors - DAY (Scene 100 & 102) 5/8
INT. Martin's Office - DAY (Scene 101) 1-1/8
Total - 3-2/8 pages.

As you can see, we are moving toward a specific area—the Director's Office. We are completing scenes within the building complex before moving on to the next area. This is an over-three page day, but most of the work is dialogue between two actors. A new character, Martin (Harrison Ford) begins today. If for any reason we were unable to do the elevator sequences the day before, we would have kept Mr. C. and Martin on alert and used these scenes as a cover set.

95

## DAY 16
### Friday, December 15

INT. Director's Office - DAY (206–221) 7-3/8
INT. Director's Office - DAY (223, 224) 4/8
INT. Elevator - DAY (225) 3/8
Total - 8-2/8

We are in the last location inside the Financial Plaza Building: the Director's office. Here, with the exception of the flashback scene (Union Square - 3/8) which we did on Day 7, this entire sequence is played in this office location among the three actors. The page count is 8-2/8 pages—the most we have scheduled so far to be completed in one day. If you had a proper rehearsal period in pre-production, plus a rehearsal the day before, and, if the director is prepared, you should be able to do all this work in one day.

If at all possible, you should always try to get the director to lay out the next day's work if this can be done with a minimum of overtime or any at all on those crew members who should remain after the camera is WRAPPED for the day.

We are about to begin the last week before Christmas. Remembering the script, we are going to have a scene in which Harry destroys his apartment looking for a supposed "bug." In order for him to be able to destroy that apartment, a false one will have to be constructed inside. This will take some time. Therefore, we should try to finish all the scenes which take place inside Harry's apartment before that. If we wait until after Christmas to do this, we may not have enough time. Therefore, we should schedule that this week. We have also found out that the location for the attorney's office is only available on Monday. Figuring that we will need at least two days to complete Harry's apartment, that leaves us only with two days before the

Christmas break. Starting any of the large scenes doesn't make any sense. Therefore, we shall fill in the rest of this week with our other small scenes—the Confessional, the Telephone Booth, the Neighborhood Laundry, etc.

## DAY 17
### Monday, December 18

INT. Lawyer's Office - Brokerage House - DAY (93, 94) 2-3/8
INT. McNaught's Office - DAY (95) 2-7/8
Total - 5-2/8 pages.

### Scenes 93, 94
Supposedly representing the apartment tenants, Harry goes to see the attorney, McNaught, to discuss making repairs on the building where he lives. We discover that Harry is secretly the landlord and wants McNaught to stall as he has done in the past. Harry hopes to sell the building to the city.

### Scene 95
Harry talks with his niece, Tony, about the problems of growing up. For the first time, we see compassion in his character.

## DAY 18
### Tuesday, December 19

INT. Harry's Apt. - DAY (40, 41) 1-3/8
Total - 1-3/8 pages

Again, beginning with the lowest scene number, Harry walks into the hallway and checks his mail. He goes into his apartment and, after discovering that Mrs. Evangelista has left a bottle of wine for his birthday, calls her. These two scenes are only 1-3/8 long. Why would we schedule an entire day for this seemingly small amount of work? Well, when you move into a location for the first day, it will take some time in the morning to move your equipment in. From the script we can tell that Harry's apartment is on an upper floor, so you will lose some time having to move equipment up via the stairs and the service elevator. Also, this location will probably not have enough power to operate all the equipment. Therefore, you are going to have to bring in your own generator and run electrical cables. This is not uncommon practice when filming in older buildings. This probably would have happened at Amy's apartment location also.

## DAY 19
### Wednesday, December 20
INT. Harry's Apt. - NIGHT (42, 43, 44) 5-7/8


Harry is interrupted while cooking his dinner. As you read, you find that the stove he is using is PRACTICAL—it actually works. Several of his neighbors join him as they discuss the lack of running water. Harry tries to maneuver the neighbors out of his apartment—but is confronted with a spontaneously provided birthday cake. All this action takes place in Harry's kitchen, living room by the front door and in the hallway. We begin the scene with one actor and end with five. The director may want coverage on them all, which takes time.

## DAY 20
### Thursday - December 21
EXT. Harry's Apt. - DAY (49) 1/8
INT. Harry's Apt. - NIGHT (48) 3/8
INT. Harry's Apt. - NIGHT (377–379) 3 pages
Total - 3-4/8 pages

## Scene 49

When shooting at a location, it is a good idea to try to finish the exteriors before doing the interiors. While you are shooting the exteriors, the crew can be inside finishing up the preparations of the interior. In this instance, it will mean re-dressing the windows for a "night" look.

## Scene 48

After finishing Scene 49, we move back inside Harry's apartment for night interiors. As the windows will have been dressed, we will shoot these night interiors during the day time.

## Scenes 377, 378, 379

Following this, we can go into the long dialogue sequence between Harry and the tenants, and then Harry talking on the phone with Mark. When we finish these three scenes, we will have completed everything we need to do at Harry's apartment except for the end scenes when he tears the place apart. The Art Department will begin construction on the false walls and floor which Harry will eventually destroy. I would allow at least two weeks for the Art Department to complete their work. Keep in mind that in the real world out there, it is five days before Christmas and everything takes that much longer to do.

## DAY 21
### Friday, December 22

EXT. Telephone Booth - DAY (92) 1-1/8
INT. Catholic Church - DAY (230, 231) 6/8
INT. Laundry - DAY (39) 5/8
INT. Hotel Auditorium - NIGHT (120, 123, 125) 6/8

## Scene 92

The day begins outside in a street telephone booth. If possible, this telephone booth should be set up around the corner from the Catholic Church so as to avoid moving the crew needlessly and allowing them to finish prepping the Church while this is being shot.

**Scenes 230, 231**
The company goes to the Catholic Church. Here Harry moves from the church pews to inside the confessional. This sequence should go very quickly as it involves only one actor - Harry.

**Scene 39**
Harry shows a little boy a magic trick. This scene is in a confined area with three actors. You will probably be dealing with overhead flourescent lights which will have to be replaced as we did in the market. They are the wrong color temperature and will give everything a strange look if not changed. Depending on the number of lights, this should be done before the shooting crew arrives.

**Scenes 120 (part), 123, 125**
To finish out the day and the week, it makes sense to schedule the three insert shots which will be needed for the St. Francis Hotel Auditorium/Convention. These three shots are actually slides which need to be prepared. Since these scenes involve none of the principal actors, they will be free to go early while still completing a good day's work.

We have now finished our last day of shooting before Christmas. The production company has a choice—either continue shooting during the Holidays, or shut down, let everyone go home and then come back rested and ready to start on Wednesday, January 3. If you are faced with having to shoot around Christmas time, if at all possible, try to arrange your schedule so that you will be able to give your crew some time off. Most everyone will go off salary during that time, although you will still have some overhead costs to maintain. Your crew should be rested and ready to begin the second half of the picture. The period between Christmas and New Year's is usually the least productive period during the year. If you can avoid shooting during this time, you should. In the instance of "The Conversation," the crew elected to go off payroll and take the time off.

## DAY 22
### Wednesday, January 3

EXT. Continental Lodge - DAY (232–236) 5/8
INT. Continental Lodge Lobby - DAY (237) 3/8
INT. Continental Lodge Corridor - DAY (238) 2/8
INT. Continental Lodge Corridor - DAY (254) 1/8
Total - 1-3/8 pages

A new year and a new location. We go to the Continental Lodge. Again, follow the exteriors first rule and try to keep in sequential order.

### Scenes 232-236
Scene 232 is actually a second unit shot as it involves no principal actors. But since it doesn't make sense to send a Second Unit back here to get a quick 1/8 of a page shot of the motel sign, we shall do this shot before we ask Harry to be on the set. Scenes 233–236 are either of Harry or are Harry's POV of the motel. Harry's POV shots will be scheduled and shot first, and then Harry will be called on to the set to shoot the other scenes.

### Scene 237
Harry walks in and asks for a particular room. This involves dialogue and two actors and shouldn't take much time to shoot.

### Scene 238
Harry arrives at his room and enters.

### Scene 254
This corridor scene needs to be shot at night. Depending on which motel has been chosen, it is possible that the corridor is

outside which would make shooting day-for-night difficult at best. Hopefully, because we are shooting in winter and it gets dark very early, we will be able to get this night shot without having to stay too long. Otherwise, we may have to create the illusion of night time.

Remembering that you have now had almost ten days off, it would be a good idea, if time allows, to block and rehearse the following day's work which has Harry entering the motel room. It's also possible that the crew would have time to pre-light the room.

## DAY 23
### Thursday, January 4

INT. Cont. Lodge Bedroom B-5 - DAY (239, 240) 2/8
INT. Cont. Lodge Bathroom B-5 - DAY (241–244) 1-1/8
INT. Cont. Lodge Bedroom B-5 DAY (245–250) 1 page
INT. Cont. Lodge Bedroom B-5 - NIGHT (251–253) 3/8
Total - 2-6/8 pages

You will note that the bedroom and bathroom scenes can be scheduled together as one location. The way it lays out in the script, you go from bedroom to bathroom and then back to the bedroom. This could be considered a double move (back to the bedroom). Actually, the whole motel room is one set. The bathrooms of most motels are small and require little preparation time (changing and setting some lights). Harry checks out the room and his neighbors in B-7 by going out onto his little terrace. In the bathroom, he begins to eavesdrop on the conversation next door. He believes that he hears Mr. C. killing Ann and Mark. In terror, he runs and hides under the bedcovers and turns the TV on to block out the murderous screams. He awakens at night and turns off the TV. Despite the fact that this scene requires only one actor and no dialogue, it will take some time because your action takes place within three specific areas in the motel room. Your director will probably want a lot of coverage to be able to create suspense. Most likely, the first three scenes will be scheduled and finished as it gets dark so that the Night Bedroom scene can be shot. Otherwise, the room windows will have to be dressed for night.

## DAY 24
### Friday, January 5

INT. Cont. Lodge Bedroom B-7 - NIGHT (255–260) - 1 page
INT. Cont. Lodge Bathroom B-7 - NIGHT (261–268) 1-3/8
EXT. Cont. Lodge - NIGHT (270) - 1/8
INT. Cont. Lodge Bathroom - NIGHT - (354) 1/8
INT. Cont. Lodge Bedroom - NIGHT - (269) 1/8
Total - 2-6/8 pages.

As this is a Friday, we can shoot all these scenes night-for-night as they are written, finish late and not worry about shooting early on Saturday. The crew's next call will be for Monday.

**Scenes 255–260, 261–268, 270, 354, 269**
Harry walks through the immaculately cleaned motel room. He finally discovers the clogged toilet which backs up—spilling bloody water onto the tile floor and then onto his shoes. The toilet backing up is a Special Effects shot which will have to be set up before hand. Although the page count for this day is only 2-6/8 pages, we are shooting at night, have many set-ups and some special effects work. This will be a good night's work.

## DAY 25
### Monday, January 8

INT. Cont. Lodge - Bedroom B-7 - DAY (363) 2/8
INT. Cont. Lodge - Bedroom B-7 - DAY (359–361) 1 page

INT. Cont. Lodge - Bathroom B-7 - DAY (356) 4/8
Total - 1-6/8 pages

You will notice right away that we have not scheduled these scenes to be shot in sequential order. Why? The nature of the scenes make it better for us to start with a clean set and then get bloody. In reality, after reading these scenes, you will see that although this shooting order is not chronological, it actually is in the correct time order. Mr. C. plays the tape for Ann and Mark. Next, Mark locks the door. They do this before they stab him. Then we see Ann and Mark stab Mr. C. in Scenes 359–361 and then, finally in Scene 356, we see them cleaning up the blood as Mr. C. lies dead. Coppola purposely juxtaposed the scenes to give you the impression that you are "seeing" what happened in the room through Harry's interpretation of the taped conversation.

When we finish today's work, we will have finished Mr. C. and Mark's work for the picture. Look back over your schedule. The last day that we used Mark was (Day 15) and the last day we used Mr. C. was (Day 16). Now count the days off (including the Christmas vacation). As you can see, enough time lapsed between their last day's work and this so that we could drop and pick up both the actors. So as not to have any actors waiting to work, it would be advisable to see if we can complete Ann's work as soon as possible. Both Stanley and Paul were dropped on Day 10 and won't be picked up until later in the schedule.

### DAYS 26 & 27
### Tuesday, January 9 & Wednesday, January 10

EXT/INT - Bus - DAY (284, 285, 289, 291) 4/8
INT. Bus - DAY (298, 300, 301, 302) 1-3/8
EXT. Bus - LATE DAY (299) 1/8

EXT. Bus - NIGHT (303, 304) 2/8
INT. Bus - NIGHT (305, 306) 1-6/8
EXT. Bus and Street - NIGHT (307, 308) 3/8
INT. Bus & Street - DAY (287, 288, 292, 293, 295, 296) 7/8
EXT. Poles and Lines (Inserts) - DAY (286, 290, 294) 3/8
EXT. Street & Harry's Bus - DAY (297) 1/8
Total - 5-6/8 pages

Look back at your schedule. On Day 4 we had Ann and Harry on the Electric Buses then. Why didn't we continue with them? Read closely and you will see that the scene is not really taking place on the bus. Harry follows Ann as she walks from the Plaza and boards a bus and then he boards one behind. We really don't get inside the bus with Ann and Harry. Harry has also been in buses on Day 2 and on Day 3. We really have to look at the Electric Bus sequences as separate locations. The main scheduling problem is to finish the Union Square sequence in time so that the sound tapes are ready to playback in the Warehouse sequence. The few short Electric Bus scenes which we scheduled earlier fit into the schedule and were not difficult to do. This sequence, however, is going to take us at least two days to shoot.

We begin this sequence in the daytime, move into the late afternoon and continue into the evening. Looking at the material you have left to schedule, you can see that we are going to be in for a few evenings of night shooting. The change from day to night occurs in Scene 303 with an Exterior Shot of the Bus in which they are riding. After reading over the material, you realize that this is a lot of material to cover which requires much action and a dramatic conflict between the two main actors. Harry is going to be jumping in and out of buses— running from one to another. Because of the added difficulties of shooting at night, we have scheduled this over two days (nights). We shall continue with the night work so that we can finish Ann. What will happen most likely is that we will begin shooting the day/late day sequences, finish some of the night work, return the next day late in the afternoon with Harry alone to do his scenes (beginning with Scene 287), do the inserts and then Scene 297 making this second day a fairly short day/night.

## DAY 28
### Thursday, January 11

EXT. Stepped Street - NIGHT (309–316) 1-1/8
EXT. The Park - NIGHT (317–332) 4-3/8
Total - 5-4/8 pages

**Scenes 309–316**
We see Harry pursuing Ann down the streets. It makes most sense to begin with Ann's scenes first and shoot all of hers, and then begin the SINGLES on Harry. This is the director's decision, so we are leaving the option up to him. This night's work could be shot with a hand-held camera.

**Scenes 317–332**
Harry follows Ann into a multi-level park. He pours out his innermost feelings to her in an effort to purge his guilt. Together, these two sequences are 5-4/8 pages long. Why do we think that we can do this in one night when the same amount of material took two days' before (Tuesday & Wednesday)? Well, first you have very little dialogue. From Scene 309 on to Scene 332, Ann has one line of dialogue, *"Please leave me alone."* Harry does all the talking. Secondly, you have very few locations involved. The main location is in the park and Harry walks along the first level delivering his lines, ending up sitting on a small bench. If the actors have been able to rehearse the

scene in pre-production, then we should be able to accomplish this work in one night.

When we do, Ann will have completed all her work on this picture and be done.

## DAY 29
### Friday, January 12

INT. Harry's Apartment - NIGHT (380–397) 2-7/8
Total - 2-7/8 pages.

The Art Department and Construction Department should have had enough time to re-dress this apartment and construct the false walls and floor which Harry will rip out. It is one thing to take a telephone apart or remove an electrical wall plate, and entirely another to steam off wall paper and pull up the wooden floor. In the script, Harry does not tear into the walls or the floor. Francis Coppola decided that it would be a good idea to convey the character's total desperation and helplessness. After reading the 2-7/8 pages, it becomes obvious that it would take an entire day (or night) of shooting to get all the necessary shots for this sequence. If this isn't planned properly, it will take longer. Since this is a night sequence and since you are on location with windows which could look out to the world, it should be scheduled at night.

## DAYS 30 & 31
### Monday, January 13 & Tuesday, January 14

EXT. Harry's Warehouse - DAY (50) 2/8
INT. Harry's Warehouse - DAY (51–57, 59–61, 63, 65, 67, 69, 70, 72–80, 82–86, 88–91) 11-6/8
Total - 9-3/8 pages

As we now begin our seventh week, you can see that we have established a clear pattern of grouping our day work and our night work and trying to shoot in sequential order at a location. We try to schedule all the night work for the latter part of the week. This week we are going to begin the Harry's Warehouse sequence. This is a classic example of good scheduling by Clark Paylow, the production manager on THE CONVERSATION. Harry's warehouse is, most likely, an actual location and not a built set. It will probably be a large warehouse with large windows made of safety glass. Unless there is an area within the warehouse which can be shielded from the windows, you are going to feel as if you are shooting in a fishbowl and will be at the mercy of the sun. You will probably have to shoot what is called for in the script—day-for-day and night-for-night without faking it.

**Scene 50**
Harry walks along the exterior of his place of business. This is the first and only time we see the Warehouse exterior in the day time.

**Scenes 51–57**
We move inside to where Harry begins analyzing his tapes.

**Scenes 59–61**
We see Harry operate the recording equipment professionally. This is very easy to say, but will require many hours of rehearsal time which shall have to be scheduled most likely during pre-production. We will need to have copies of the conversation which Harry taped in Union Square to play back during these scenes. Stanley is now in these scenes. We pick him up again after dropping him on Day 10.

**Scene 63, 65, 67**
Trying to shoot in sequential order as much as possible because of the potential light problem, we now schedule the disagree-

ment between Stanley and Harry. Stanley leaves for lunch in a huff. Harry continues to work.

## Scenes 69, 70, 72–80
Alone, Harry continues to work on the tapes. We watch him as he professionally works the dials and switches. He uses some of his homemade equipment to further decipher the tapes.

## Scenes 82–86
Harry checks the results. He has filtered out most of the static and has added more meaning to their conversation.

## Scenes 88–91
Harry pushes the rewind button, looks at the tape and then at the still photographs of Ann and Mark.

By finishing this sequence, we have completed 11-3/8 pages of work in two days. As you can see from the scenes, we are doing a lot of coverage of the equipment working. Also, we have now completed all the daytime work at this location and shall move into three day's of night work.

### DAYS 32, 33, & 34
### Wednesday, January 15; Thursday, January 16, Friday January 17.
INT. Harry's Warehouse - NIGHT (160–173) 19-4/8

This sequence begins with a dark warehouse and then the group from the St. Francis Hotel arriving for the impromptu party. In the next thirteen scenes, you have seven actors working. Once we begin these actors, we will concentrate on keeping their schedules tight so that we can finish them quickly. More than five pages of this entire sequence involves Harry and Meredith dancing and talking (Scenes 161–164). Approximately seven pages involves Harry and Moran engaged in conversation with most of the others joining in (Scenes 164–173). This part of the sequence occurs in and out of the caged area where Harry keeps his personal equipment. We are looking at shooting an entire sequence which runs 19-4/8 pages. It should be obvious that we cannot attempt this in one or even two days. With a rehearsal and time to block the action beforehand, we should be able to finish this in three long, hard days. If we run into any problems, we can always go into a fourth day.

## DAYS 35 & 36
### Monday, January 20; Tuesday, January 21

INT. Harry's Warehouse - NIGHT (174–181, 183–184, 186, 187) 10-6/8
Total - 10-6/8 pages

We continue shooting night for night. We continue where we left off with Harry and Meredith. The others have left the party and now Harry and Meredith continue talking. Judging from the page count (10-6/8 pages), the movement within the warehouse, and the amount of dialogue between the two, this is going to require two day's (night's) work.

## DAY 37
### Wednesday, January 22

INT. Harry's Warehouse - NIGHT (337–353, 355, 357–358, 362, 364) 4-6/8
EXT. Harry's Warehouse - NIGHT (333–336) 4/8
Total - 5-2/8 pages

Why are we breaking rules—shooting out of sequence and not shooting the exteriors first? Since we are already set up inside, to stop now and shoot exteriors would mean moving all the equipment outside, only to move it back inside again. We don't need to have a double move. Plus, while we are finishing up inside, the rest of the crew can be setting up lights for the exteriors.

After completing the interior work which is the major portion of the work (5-4/8 pages), we can begin to partially STRIKE the inside set (location), removing any equipment which we will not need. If the ceiling is pre-rigged, then the equipment should not be removed until after the DAILIES have been seen and approved.

Harry discovers that someone is breaking into his warehouse as he arrives. He scares the burglars away. Before they leave, they turn on his tape recorder. Harry listens to the tape again and discovers a new meaning to Ann's line, *"Do you think we can do it?"*

From Harry's point of view (POV) he sees two men. We don't actually see them. The majority of tonight's work is on Harry. We should be able to finish it in one night.

## DAY 38
### Thursday, January 23

INT. - Staff Car - NIGHT (Scenes 144, 146 - 6/8)
INT/EXT. - Staff Car - NIGHT (Scenes 147, 148 - 2/8)
INT/EXT. - Staff Car - NIGHT (Scene 149 - 3/8)
INT. - Staff Car - NIGHT (Scenes 151, 152, 153, 155 - 6/8)
INT. - Staff Car - NIGHT (Scenes 157, 158 - 2/8)
INT. - Staff Car - NIGHT (Scene 159- 1/8)

EXT. - Street/Mustang - NIGHT (Scenes 145, 150, 154, 156
- 4/8)
Total - 3 pages

Properly planned, this night driving sequence can be finished in one evening. Through careful reading, it is a driving and dialogue sequence, not a stunt/chase sequence. Only one time does the driver of the Mustang almost lose control of this car (Scene 150 - Stunt). The Mustang Driver has only one line which he delivers while sitting at a stop light. Therefore, you are placing your emphasis on the Staff Car. In order to cut down on the time needed to make the vehicle ready for filming (installing FRONT and SIDE CAR MOUNTS for the camera, and possibly a battery pack in the trunk to provide power for the lights needed to shoot the interior of the car) you should have more than one car available. The duplicate Staff Car could be pre-rigged with car mounts—special devices which hold the 35mm camera on a platform—in place. Other mounts, then, are used to hold the lights inside the car. These car mounts can be put on any number of places on the car. The most common placement is on the side of the car and on the hood. We explain this to you now because most of this sequence will be shot with the use of car mounts. In addition to the platforms, a CAMERA CAR will probably also be used as well as RUN-BYS (shots of the car driving by a stationary camera). To play it safe, it would be a good idea to duplicate the Mustang, too. If anything should happen to either vehicle (mechanical failure, accident, etc.) you wouldn't lose any time. When you are spending well over $70,000 per night for night shooting, a stand-by car is inexpensive insurance. You might find that this material should be shot using PROCESS SHOTS. The car itself would be placed on a sound stage and film of a moving background would be projected onto a transparent screen behind. In this case, the director chose to shoot everything on location.

## DAY 39
### Friday, January 24

INT. Hotel Convention Bar - NIGHT (133–136) - 1-5/8
INT. Hotel Convention - NIGHT (137–142) 4-3/8
EXT. Hotel Convention - NIGHT (143) 6/8
Total - 6-6/8 pages

Since Thursday was a night call, we must continue with, at best, a late afternoon crew call.

### Scenes 133–136
Harry tries to make a phone call, hangs up and runs into Martin from Mr. C's office.

### Scenes 137–142
We pick up Harry, inside the convention center, being hustled over to Moran's booth. Moran has placed a bug in the Ladies' room and they are all eavesdropping. Meredith and Lurleen join the boys as they head for the door. This sequence has two key filming areas—by Moran's booth and by the Ladies' room. In the rehearsal period and on the location scout, this scene should be laid out and blocked in advance.

### Scene 143
If you were able to give your crew a late afternoon call, then it is probably dark enough outside to do the Parking Lot scene. Although it is Friday night and everyone is tired after almost 1-1/2 weeks of night shooting, we are going to try to finish this scene tonight. It isn't too long or very difficult. Here you will be able to control the vehicle and pedestrian traffic outside in the hotel parking lot. Once you get the Master Shot of all of them trying to get into the car and, possibly, driving off, the

coverage should be fairly easy to control. While you were inside doing the previous scenes, part of your crew should be out here setting up for this scene. It should be obvious to you that we did our interiors here first so that we could finish Friday evening with a night exterior.

## DAY 40
### Monday, January 27

INT. Hotel Convention - NIGHT (109–120-part) 2-3/8
INT. Hotel Auditorium - NIGHT (121–122, 124) 1-5/8
Total - 4 pages

**Scenes 109–120-part**
Having completed the night exterior on Friday, we can go back to sequential shooting beginning with the first scene scheduled for this location. Depending on the location and the amount of daylight you actually see from the convention room, you should be able to shoot this day-for-night.

The opening sequence establishes the convention. With the number of extras you are going to have, it will take longer to shoot this sequence. We bring back Martin. He is at the Convention to see Harry.

**Scenes 121, 122, 124**
Having scheduled and completed part of Scene 120 as well as Scenes 123 and 125 on Day 21, the slide show presentation coverage is already done. That leaves us to focus on Harry entering the auditorium and looking around. Your extras are watching the activity, so there shouldn't be too much coordination. Paul greets Harry.

## DAY 41
### Tuesday, January 28

INT. Hotel Convention Center - Main Room - NIGHT (126–132) 8-7/8

Harry and Paul enter the main room where the exhibit booths are located. Harry, Moran, and Meredith meet. This is a long sequence—almost nine pages long, but over half of it involves Moran giving a stand-up demonstration of his surveillance device. Harry moves on and discusses equipment with another dealer from Elco Electronics. These two areas within the main convention center room should be rehearsed and blocked. The result would be being able to complete close to seven pages in this, the last day of shooting.

One last bit of advice before moving onto the shooting schedule, if at all possible when working on a production as a production manager or first assistant director, try always to get your director to lay out the next day's work if it can be done with a minimum of overtime, or any at all, on those crew members who should remain after the camera is wrapped for the day. This will help immeasurably when you find yourself up against a tight schedule.

Well, congratulate yourself. You have just made it through the breakdown and scheduling of a feature film. Study the Production Board. Make sure you understand the reasons THE CONVERSATION was scheduled this way. I hope that many of you have gone along and prepared your own color-coded board as an exercise. As I stressed before, the best way to learn how to schedule a film is to do it!

# IX

## THE SHOOTING SCHEDULE

A SHOOTING SCHEDULE is another production board, only typed on a form. Sometimes only a little information is listed, sometimes more. The schedule will be handed out to all the cast and crew. Revisions of the shooting schedule should be handed out just as soon as they are available. Using a different color paper and dating the sheets will make it easy to know which is the most current. The schedule will give the cast and crew a projection of how the show is laid out and when certain scenes have been scheduled.

In order to make sure that all pertinent information is listed on the shooting schedule, it is a good idea to go over the breakdown sheet and see what else should be included. Special equipment, wardrobe, stunt doubles, etc., which might not appear on the production strip board due to lack of space are on the breakdown sheets and should appear on the shooting schedule. Also, have your marked up script handy to double-check any last minute questions which might arise.

Now, please turn to the Shooting Schedule on the following pages.

## SHOOTING SCHEDULE

## FRANCIS FORD COPPOLA PRODS.

TITLE: **THE CONVERSATION**                    PRODUCERS:  F. F. COPPOLA
                                                            F. ROOS
SHOOTING DATES: 11/26/-- THRU                               M. SKAGER
                1/30/--                         DIRECTOR:   F. F. COPPOLA
                                                PROD. MGR:  CLARK PAYLOW
                                                ASST. DIR.  C. MYERS
TOTAL PAGES: 157

| DAY/DATE | SET/SCENES | CAST/ATMOS | STAGE/LOCATION |
|---|---|---|---|
| DAY 1 SUNDAY 11/26/-- | **EXT. FINANCIAL DISTRICT (SUNDAY) (D)** | #1 - HARRY | #1 EMBARCADERO BUILDING |
| 3-4/8 | Scenes: 195-198 5/8 | EXTRAS: Uniformed Sec. Guard | PROPS Blue Pouch Gun For Guard Clipboard |
| | Harry through Sunday Streets, signs in goes up. | | |

| DAY/DATE | SET/SCENES | CAST/ATMOS | STAGE/LOCATION |
|---|---|---|---|
| DAY 1 cont'd. | **EXT. FINANCIAL DIST. (PHONE BOOTH) (D)** | #1 - HARRY | PROPS Blue Pouch (Empty) |
| | Scenes: 226-229 4/8 | | |
| | Harry at loose ends, gets into phone booth. | | |
| | COMPANY MOVES TO GOLDEN GATE PARK (BANDSTAND AREA) | | |
| | **EXT. GOLDEN GATE PARK (D)** | #1 - HARRY #5 - STAN | EXT. G/G PARK |
| | Scenes: 188-194 2-3/8 | EXTRAS Old Woman in Park | PROPS Blue Pouch |
| | Harry accosts Stan. Tells him that Meredith has gone through his things. Tells him to stay away from him. | MEN IN SUITS TO PASS OUT PROGRAMS. GEN. ATMOS. | MUSIC BAND |
| | END OF FIRST DAY | | |

119

| DAY/DATE | SET/SCENES | CAST/ATMOS | STAGE/LOCATION |
|---|---|---|---|
| DAY 2 MONDAY 11/27/-- | **EXT. STREET/ELECT. BUS/NEIGHBORHOOD (D)** | #1 - HARRY | FILLMORE & HAYES STREET - YOUNG'S FOOD MART |
| 6/8 | Scene 34, 36, 37 3/8 | <u>EXTRAS</u> Bus Driver #1 | <u>EFX</u> Sparks from Bus. |
| | Scene 34 - Electric Bus travels up street (1/8) | Atmos. on Bus. | |
| | Scene 36 - Driver fixes rod, Harry walks toward his home. (1/8) | | |
| | Scene 37 - Bus passes Harry. (1/8) | | |

| DAY/DATE | SET/SCENES | CAST/ATMOS | STAGE/LOCATION |
|---|---|---|---|
| DAY 2 cont'd. | **INT. ELECT. BUS (D)** Scene 35 2/8 | EXTRAS Bus Driver #1 | PROPS Packages, Brief-cases, etc. for passengers. |
| | Harry on bus. driver off to fix rod. Harry gets off | Atmos. on Bus | |
| | **INT. MARKET (D)** Scene 38 1/8th | #1 - HARRY | PROPS Tomato, Pork Chops (in cellophane), can of beer, money, sack/purchases. |
| | | EXTRAS Counter Man (clerk) Others, if needed. | |
| | Harry shops. | | |

END OF SECOND DAY

121

| DAY/DATE | SET/SCENES | CAST/ATMOS | STAGE/LOCATION |
|---|---|---|---|
| DAY 3 TUESDAY 11/28/-- 2/8 | EXT. STREET (D) (Burning Car) Scene 365 1/8 Mr. C and car go up up in flames | #4 - MR. C (Stunt Dbl?) | PROPS Blood on Mr. C. EFX Car Burns |
| | INT./EXT. ELECT. BUS & STREET (N) Scene 45 1/8 Harry w/wine on bus. | #1 - HARRY EXTRAS Bus Driver #2 Few atmos. on bus. | LOCATION #2 PROPS Bottle/Wine |

END OF THIRD DAY

| DAY/DATE | SET/SCENES | CAST/ATMOS | STAGE/LOCATION |
| --- | --- | --- | --- |
| DAY 4 WEDNESDAY 11/29/-- | **EXT. FINANCIAL DISTRICT (D)** | #1 - HARRY | SANSOME & CALIF. STREETS |
| 7/8 | Scenes 96, 97 2/8 | EXTRAS Gen. atmos on street (25) | PROPS Blue Pouch |
|  | Harry heads for Mr. C.'s office. |  |  |
|  | **EXT. FINANCIAL PLAZA (D)** | #1 - HARRY | PROPS Attache Case |
|  | Scenes 272, 272 2/8 | EXTRAS Atmos. (75) |  |
|  | Harry heads through work day crowds for Mr. C. |  |  |
|  | COMPANY MOVES TO #1 EMBARCADERO - CLAY ST. ALCOA PLAZA |  |  |

| DAY/DATE | SET/SCENES | CAST/ATMOS | STAGE/LOCATION |
|---|---|---|---|
| DAY 4 cont'd. | **EXT. DIRECTOR'S BLDG. (BUS #1 & #2)** <br> **(D)** | #1 - HARRY <br> #2 - ANN <br> #37-DRIVER (Bus #1) <br> #38-DRIVER (Bus #2) | #1 EMBARCADERO <br> CLAY ST/ALCOA PL. |
| | Scenes 282, 283 3/8 | EXTRAS <br> Passengers on both buses. | PROPS <br> 2 Elect. Trolleys <br> Attache Case |
| | Ann gets onto bus, Harry follow on second bus. | | EFX <br> Fog? |

END OF FOURTH DAY

| DAY/DATE | SET/SCENES | CAST/ATMOS | STAGE/LOCATION |
|---|---|---|---|
| DAYS 5&6 THURSDAY 11/30-- FRIDAY, 12/1/-- | **EXT.  UNION SQUARE (D)** Scenes 1-9, 3-1/8th | # 1 - HARRY # 2 - ANN # 3 - MARK #6  - PAUL #21 - MIME #22 - YNG MAN #23 - YNG WOM | UNION SQUARE <br> PROPS Lunch for Mark Coffee in sack for Harry Mirror van w/sign "Bay Cities Glass & Mirror Co." Shotgun Microphone w/telescopic sight Earphones Paper Bag and Hearing Aid-Paul |
| 6-7/8 | Establishes Union Square.  Harry drinks coffee & watches Ann and Mark talk. Harry moves from bench to van.  Pan to Man w/ microphone on top of City of Paris Bldg. | ST. ATMOS Derelict Eiffel Tower Man Street Band | MUSIC Street Band - "Red Red Robin." |

125

| DAY/DATE | SET/SCENES | CAST/ATMOS | STAGE/LOCATION |
|---|---|---|---|
| DAYS 5 & 6 cont'd | **EXT. UNION SQ. (D)** **(FTG FOR WRHSE. SEQ.)** | # 2 – ANN<br># 3 – MARK<br># 6 – PAUL<br>#21 – MIME | PROPS<br>Lunch Sack<br>Mirror Van<br>Sack & Hearing Aid |
| | Scenes: 58, 62, 64, 66, 68, 71, 87, 107 3-4/8 | | |
| | Scene 58 (5/8) Fragment conv. Mark/Ann | EXTRAS<br>Derelict<br>Street Band | MUSIC<br>Red Red Robin |
| | Scene 62 (3/8) Mark & Ann talk about gift. | ATMOS<br>Gen. Street. | NOTE<br>Repeat footage sequences |
| | Scene 64 (1/8) View of Derelict. | | |

126

| DAY/DATE | SET/SCENES | CAST/ATMOS | STAGE/LOCATION |
|---|---|---|---|
| DAYS 5 & 6 cont'd. | Scene 66 (3/8) Ann & Mark walk past derelict. | | |
| | Scene 68 (7/8) Ann & Mark talk – Mime. | | |
| | Scene 71 (4/8) Ann spots Paul. | | |
| | Scene 87 (4/8) Ann & Mark kiss goodbye. | | |
| | Scene 107 (1/8) Ann & Mark kiss goodbye. | | |

END OF FIFTH & SIXTH DAYS -- END OF FIRST WEEK

| DAY/DATE | SET/SCENES | CAST/ATMOS | STAGE/LOCATION |
|---|---|---|---|
| DAY 7 MONDAY 12/4/-- | **EXT. UNION SQ. (D)** Scenes 19-22 1-1/8 | # 2 – ANN # 3 – MARK # 6 – PAUL #21 – MIME #24 – SHOPPER #1 #25 – SHOPPER #2 #26 – SHOPPER #3 | UNION SQUARE PROPS Lunch Bag Paper Bag Hearing Aid |
| 2-4/8 | Ann & Mark continue walking. Paul trails behind; they spot him. He leaves. | EXTRAS Street Atmos. | Hearing Aid |
| | **EXT. UNION SQ. (D)** Scene 81 3/8 | # 2 – ANN # 3 – MARK | MUSIC Red Red Robin |
| | Mark's voice distorts, "kill us." | EXTRAS Bongo Players Street Atmos. | |

| DAY/DATE | SET/SCENES | CAST/ATMOS | STAGE/LOCATION |
|---|---|---|---|
| DAY 7 cont'd. | **<u>EXT. UNION SQ. (D)</u>**<br><br>Scenes 28, 33 3/8<br><br>Scene 28 (2/8) Ann & part company. Derelict awakens, Mark throws away sack & leaves.<br><br>Scene 33 (1/8) – Musicians pack up. | # 2 – ANN<br># 3 – MARK<br>#21 – MIME<br><br><u>EXTRAS</u><br>Derelict<br>Street Atmos.<br>(thinning out) | <u>MUSIC</u><br>Red, Red Robin<br><br><u>PROPS</u><br>Lunch sack/Mark |

129

| DAY/DATE | SET/SCENES | CAST/ATMOS | STAGE/LOCATION |
|---|---|---|---|
| DAY 7 cont'd. | **EXT. UNION SQ. (D)** <br> **(SUPER O/WHSE SEQ.)** <br><br> Scenes 182, 185 <br> 2/8 <br><br> Scene 182 (1/8) Mark and Ann circle park. <br><br> Scene 184 (1/8) Pan of terrified Ann through park. | # 2 – ANN <br> # 3 – MARK <br> #21 – MIME <br><br> EXTRAS <br> Derelict <br> Street Band <br> Atmos. | PROPS <br> Lunch sack/Mark <br><br> MUSIC <br> Red, Red Robin |

| DAY/DATE | SET/SCENES | CAST/ATMOS | STAGE/LOCATION |
|---|---|---|---|
| DAY 7 cont'd. | **EXT. UNION SQ. (D)** (PREVIOUS FOOTAGE)  Scene 222 (3/8)  Ann and Mark spot Paul. | # 2 – ANN  # 3 – MARK  # 6 – PAUL  #21 – MIME  EXTRAS  Derelict  Street Band | PROPS  Paper sack/Paul  Lunch/Mark  MUSIC |

END OF SEVENTH DAY

131

| DAY/DATE | SET/SCENES | CAST/ATMOS | STAGE/LOCATION |
|---|---|---|---|
| DAYS 8&9 TUESDAY 12/5/-- | **EXT. EIFFEL TOWER** **ROOF – (D)** | # 2 – ANN # 3 – MARK # 6 – PAUL | UNION SQUARE CITY OF PARIS |
| WEDNESDAY 12/6/-- 3-2/8 | Scenes 1Ø, 11, 25, 26, 17, 31 1-3/8 | EXTRAS Man on Roof #1 Derelict Atmos. in Sq. Street Band | PROPS Shotgun Microphone w/ earphones Nylon Bag Mirror Van Lunch/Mark Bag/Paul Bongo drums. |
| | Scenes 1Ø, 11 (3/8) Man's POV – Ann & Mark talking. | | |
| | Scene 25 (1/8) Man tracks Ann & Mark with microphone. | | |
| | Scene 26 (4/8) – Tele POV Ann & Mark near bongos. | | |

continued...

132

| DAY/DATE | SET/SCENES | CAST/ATMOS | STAGE/LOCATION |
|---|---|---|---|
| DAYS 8&9 cont'd. | **EXT. EIFFEL TOWER** <u>ROOF - (D)</u> <br><br> Scene 17 (2/8) - Pan from Man #1 to Man #2. <br> Scene 31 (1/8) - Man #1 disassembles microphone & puts in bag. | | |
| | **EXT. TOP OF BLDG.** <u>WINDOW & SQUARE - (D)</u> <br><br> Scenes 18, 23, 24, 103, 32. 1-5/8 <br><br> Scenes 18, 23 - Man tracks couple (3/8) <br><br> Scenes 24, 103 - Tele POV of Ann & Mark spot- ting Paul (1-1/8) <br><br> Scene 32 (1/8) - Man packs gear & puts away. | # 2 - ANN <br> # 3 - MARK <br> # 6 - PAUL <br> #21 - MIME <br><br> <u>EXTRAS</u> <br> Man #2 <br> Derelict <br> St. Atmos. <br> Street Band | UNION SQUARE <br><br> <u>PROPS</u> <br> Shotgun Microphone <br> Lunch Sack/Mark <br> Mirror Van <br> Paper Bag/Paul <br><br> <u>NOTE</u> <br> Repeated footage |

133

| DAY/DATE | SET/SCENES | CAST/ATMOS | STAGE/LOCATION |
|---|---|---|---|
| DAYS 8&9 cont'd. | **EXT. VAN – UNION SO. (D)**<br><br>Scenes 13, 30 (2/8)<br><br>Scene 13 – (1/8) Secretaries primp in front of mirror on van.<br><br>Scene 30 – (1/8) Van w/ laughing within. | <u>EXTRAS</u><br>2 Secretaries<br>Str. Atmos. | UNION SQUARE<br><br><u>PROPS</u><br>Mirror Van |

END OF EIGHTH AND NINTH DAYS

| DAY/DATE | SET/SCENES | CAST/ATMOS | STAGE/LOCATION |
|---|---|---|---|
| DAY 10 THURSDAY 12/7/-- | **INT. MIRROR VAN (D)** | # 1 - HARRY # 5 - STAN | UNION SQUARE OR COVER SET |
| 4-4/8 | Scene 12 4/8 | EXTRAS Atmos Outside | PROPS Eyeglasses Binoculars Coffee |
| | Stan watching tapes. Harry enters, takes up surveillance w/ binoculars. | | |
| | **INT. MIRROR VAN (D)** | # 1 - HARRY # 5 - STAN | UNION SQUARE OR COVER SET |
| | Scenes 14, 15, 16. 2-1/8 | EXTRAS Secretaries St. Atmos. | PROPS Binoculars Coffee Motorized Nikon Mirror Van |
| | Harry watches, Stan takes photos of the secretaries. Harry tells him to get back to work. Stan wonders who they are working for They check reception. | | |

135

| DAY/DATE | SET/SCENES | CAST/ATMOS | STAGE/LOCATION |
|---|---|---|---|
| DAY 10 cont'd. | **INT. MIRROR VAN (D)** | # 1 – HARRY<br># 5 – STAN<br># 6 – PAUL | UNION SQUARE |
| | Scenes 27, 29.<br>1-7/8 | | PROPS<br>Headset<br>Coffee |
| | | EXTRAS<br>St. Atmos | Shopping Bag<br>Electronic Device<br>Hearing Aid.<br>Money/Billfold |
| | Scene 27 – Paul comes into van, says he's been spotted. Harry pays him, thanks him and Paul leaves. (1-2/8) | | |
| | Scene 29 – Stan & Harry start to wrap it up. Harry makes a joke "mind your own business." (5/8) | | |

END OF THE TENTH DAY

| DAY/DATE | SET/SCENES | CAST/ATMOS | STAGE/LOCATION |
|---|---|---|---|
| DAY 11 FRIDAY 12/8/-- | **INT. AMY'S APT. BUILDING (N)** | # 1 - HARRY #16 - AMY (os) | 116 FREDERICKSON #114. |
| 5-5/8 | Scene 46 2/8 | | PROPS Wine DoorKey |
| | Harry goes to apt. Lets himself in. | | |
| | **INT. AMY'S APT. (N)** | # 1 - HARRY #16 - AMY | 116 FREDERICKSON #114 |
| | Scene 47 5-3/8 | | PROPS Wine bottle Stereo Photos on walls Rent money Wine glasses Opener |
| | Harry tells Amy it's his b'day. They toast. Amy asks questions.... Harry cuts her off. She hums song which disturbs him. He leaves her money for rent and goes. | | |

END OF ELEVENTH DAY - END OF SECOND WEEK

137

| DAY/DATE | SET/SCENES | CAST/ATMOS | STAGE/LOCATION |
|---|---|---|---|
| DAY 12 MONDAY 12/11/-- | **EXT. AMY'S BLDG (D)** | #1 - HARRY | 116 FREDERICKSON #114 |
| 1-7/8 | Scene 104 1/8th | | PROPS Pouch Key |
| | Harry rushes to Amy's. | | |
| | **INT. AMY'S APT (D)** | #1 - HARRY | 116 FREDERICKSON #114 |
| | Scenes 105, 106, 108 1-6/8 | | PROPS Pouch Money in Saucer |
| | Amy is gone, rent money untouched. Mark & Ann's conversation plays o.s. Harry is alone, upset. | | |

END OF TWELFTH DAY

| DAY/DATE | SET/SCENES | CAST/ATMOS | STAGE/LOCATION |
|---|---|---|---|
| DAY 13 TUESDAY 12/12/-- <br><br> 2-3/8 | INT. **MR.C'S BLDG.** **ELEVATOR (D)** <br><br> Scene 98 <br> 6/8 <br><br> Harry in noisy elevator. Heads for top. Conversations bother him. | #1 - HARRY <br> #29 - WOM. IN ELEVATOR #1 <br> #30 - WOM. IN ELEVATOR #2 <br> #31 - MAN IN ELEVATOR <br><br> EXTRAS <br> Uniformed Gd. <br> Gen Atmos. | #1 EMBARCADERO BLDG. <br><br> PROPS <br> Blue Pouch <br> Gun /Guard (?) <br> Briefcases <br> for atmos. |
| | INT. **ELEVATOR (D)** <br><br> Scene 199 <br> 1/8th <br><br> Harry in elevator w/ blue pouch - alone. | #1 - HARRY | PROPS <br> Blue Pouch |

| DAY/DATE | SET/SCENES | CAST/ATMOS | STAGE/LOCATION |
|---|---|---|---|
| DAY 13 cont'd | **INT. ELEVATOR (D)** | # 1 – HARRY<br># 2 – ANN | PROPS<br>Attache Case |
| | Scenes 276, 277, 280, 281 | | |
| | 7/8 | EXTRAS<br>Atmos – on & off elevator. | |
| | Harry gets into elevator. A few stops later, Ann gets on. Harry – nervous. Then they both exit. | | |
| | **INT. LOBBY – MR. C'S BLDG. – NEWSSTAND (D)** | # 1 – HARRY | PROPS<br>Newspapers – Pix of burned M-Benz & Headlines. |
| | Scenes 366, 367, 368 | EXTRAS<br>Gen Atmos<br>Sec. Guard | Blue Pouch |
| | 5/8 | | |
| | Harry looks at paper. Mr. C's on front page. | | |

END OF THIRTEENTH DAY

140

| DAY/DATE | SET/SCENES | CAST/ATMOS | STAGE/LOCATION |
|---|---|---|---|
| DAY 14 WEDNESDAY 12/13/-- 3-1/8 | **INT. MR.C'S SUITE LOBBY & CORRIDOR (D)** <br><br> Scenes 200, 201, 202 203, 204, 205 <br><br> 1 page <br><br> Harry passes janitor spots Doberman. Goes quietly to Mr. C's. | # 1 - HARRY <br><br> EXTRAS Janitor | #1 EMBARCADERO 24TH FLOOR <br><br> PROPS Trans. Radio Janitorial suppl. Blue Pouch <br><br> ANIMALS Doberman Pinscher (handler) |
| | **INT. MR. C'S SUITE RECEPTION AREA (D)** <br><br> Scenes 273, 274, 275 1-1/8 <br><br> Harry heads for Mr.C's office. Recep. tries to stop him & calls guard. Harry leaves when he sees Mr. C's not there. | # 1 - HARRY <br><br> EXTRAS Receptionist Sec. Guard Atmos. | PROPS Attache Case Gun f/Guard |

| DAY/DATE | SET/SCENES | CAST/ATMOS | STAGE/LOCATION |
|---|---|---|---|
| DAY 14 cont'd. | **INT. MR. C'S SUITE** <u>RECEPTION AREA (D)</u> | # 1 – HARRY<br># 2 – ANN<br># 3 – MARK<br># 7 – MARTIN | |
| | Scenes 369, 370, 371, 372, 373, 374, 375, 376. | <u>EXTRAS</u><br>Sec. Guard<br>Young Man<br>Atmos. "Crowd" | <u>PROPS</u><br>Blue Pouch<br>Camera f/press<br>  photogs.<br>Guns f/Guards. |
| | 1 page | | |
| | Harry & Pouch make it in time to see Ann who sees Harry and indicates to Mark that Harry knows. They leave. | | |

END OF FOURTEENTH DAY

142

| DAY/DATE | SET/SCENES | CAST/ATMOS | STAGE/LOCATION |
|---|---|---|---|
| DAY 15<br>THURSDAY<br>12/14/-- | **INT. SUITE/RECEP/**<br>**CORRIDOR/OFFICE (D)**<br><br>Scenes 99, 100, 101,<br>102.<br><br>2-6/8<br><br>3-2/8<br><br>Harry sees recep. who<br>refers him to Martin.<br>Spots Mark. Won't give<br>tape to anyone but Mr. C.<br>he leaves. Sees Mark<br>on way out. | # 1 – HARRY<br># 3 – MARK<br># 7 – MARTIN<br>#20 – MALE<br>RECEPT.<br><br>EXTRAS<br>Atmos in off. | #1 EMBARCADERO<br>41ST FLOOR<br><br><br>PROPS<br>Blue Pouch<br>PBS & TV<br>Monitors<br>Envelope w/money |

END OF FIFTEENTH DAY

143

| DAY/DATE | SET/SCENES | CAST/ATMOS | STAGE/LOCATION |
|---|---|---|---|
| DAY 16 FRIDAY 12/15/-- | **INT. MR. C'S OFF (D)** | # 1 – HARRY<br># 4 – MR. C<br># 7 – MARTIN | #1 EMBARCADERO 41ST FLOOR |
| | Scenes 206, 207, 208, 209, 210, 211, 212, 213, 214, 215, 216, 217, 218, 219, 220, 221, 223, 224, 225. | | PROPS<br>Blue Pouch w/tapes<br>Recorder<br>Money in Envelope<br>Hearing Aid. |
| 8-2/8 | 8-2/8 | | ANIMALS<br>Doberman Pinscher<br>& Handler |

Harry watches dog, sees
Mr. C. Fixes hearing aid
and turns over tapes.
Martin enters and all
listen. Tape doesn't
incriminate anyone, but
Martin is sure there is
more. They continue to
listen. Mr. C. tells

144

| DAY/DATE | SET/SCENES | CAST/ATMOS | STAGE/LOCATION |
|---|---|---|---|
| DAY 16 cont'd. | Harry that Ann is his wife. Harry is shocked -- asks many un-professional questions. Wants to know what Mr. C. is going to do. Feels responsible. Harry finally leaves. Martin tells him to forget about it. | | |

END OF SIXTEENTH DAY - END OF THIRD WEEK

145

| DAY/DATE | SET/SCENES | CAST/ATMOS | STAGE/LOCATION |
|---|---|---|---|
| DAY 17<br>MONDAY<br><br>12/18/-- | **INT. LAWYER'S OFFICE<br>(D)** | # 1 - HARRY<br>#13 - MCNAUGHT<br>#19 - TONY | PACIFIC STOCK<br>BROKERAGE CO. |
| 5-2/8 | Scenes 93, 94, 95<br>2-3/8<br>Harry meets with McNaught<br>and gives him tenants'<br>complaints. They eat<br>during dicussion. Harry<br>and McNaught are friends<br>even if they only speak<br>every once in a while.<br>Harry leaves. | | PROPS<br>Blue Pouch<br>Briefcase<br>Slip of paper from<br>tenants.<br>2 sack lunches.<br><br>OTHER<br>Teacher? |
| | Scene 95<br>2-7/8<br>Harry & Tony talk about<br>problems. She cries. | # 1 - HARRY<br>#19 - TONY | MAKE-UP<br>Tears |

END OF SEVENTEENTH DAY

| DAY/DATE | SET/SCENES | CAST/ATMOS | STAGE/LOCATION |
|---|---|---|---|
| DAY 18 TUESDAY 12/19/-- | **INT. HARRY'S APT. BUILDING (D)** | # 1 - HARRY #11 - MRS. GOETNER | 700 LAGUNA STREET #306, 307 |
| 1-3/8 | Scene 40 3/8 | | PROPS Mailbox key Bills, Ads, Postcard, Laundry Groceries |
| | Harry collects mail. Mrs. Goetner w/dog says hello, happy birthday. He says hello and goes into his apt. | | ANIMALS Dog |
| | **INT. HARRY'S APT (D)** | # 1 - HARRY | 700 LAGUNA STREET #306, 307 |
| | Scene 41 1 page | | PROPS Bottle of wine Mail (incl. post-card) Groceries. |
| | Harry finds b/day wine, card froms Mrs. Evange-lista. Gets angry at her. | | |

END OF EIGHTEENTH DAY

147

| DAY/DATE | SET/SCENES | CAST/ATMOS | STAGE/LOCATION |
|---|---|---|---|
| DAY 19 WEDNESDAY 12/20/-- | **INT. HARRY'S APT.** **LIV.RM/KITCHEN (N)** | #1 - HARRY #11 - MRS. G. #12 - RON #13 - MR. CORSITTO #14 - BOB #15 - BOB'S WIFE | 700 LAGUNA STREET #306, 307 |
| 5-7/8 | Scenes 42,43,44 5-7/8 | | PROPS Wine Bottle Laundry Mail Groceries Practical sink & stove. Pork Chops/cook) Tomato & Knife Misc. kitch.uten. Plastic madonna Cupcake w/candles. Broom, glass. |
| | Harry cooks. Hears o/s dialogue. Tries to eavesdrop w/glass. Almost gets caught by Ron. No hot water. Other tenants complain. Mrs. Goetner brings small cake w/4 candles aflame. Harry is appt'd. spokesman for tenants. They leave. | | CONSTRUCTION Pract.trap door in closet. |

END OF NINETEENTH DAY

| DAY/DATE | SET/SCENES | CAST/ATMOS | STAGE/LOCATION |
|---|---|---|---|
| DAY 20<br>THURSDAY<br>12/21/--<br><br>3-4/8 | **EXT. HARRY'S APT. (D)**<br><br>Scene 49<br>1/8<br><br>Harry exits bldg. Walks to bus stop passing demolition crew. | #1 - HARRY<br><br>EXTRAS<br>Atmos.<br>Const. Crew | 700 LAGUNA STREET<br><br>MISC<br>Construction Crew & Vehicles (?) |
| | **INT. HARRY'S APT. (N)**<br><br>Scene 48<br>3/8<br><br>Harry plays saxaphone to old recording. | # 1 - HARRY | 700 LAGUNA STREET<br>#306, 307<br><br>PROPS<br>Stereo set up as designated.<br>Saxaphone (sp?)<br><br>MISC<br>Jazz rec. to p/b. |

149

| DAY/DATE | SET/SCENES | CAST/ATMOS | STAGE/LOCATION |
|---|---|---|---|
| DAY 20 cont'd. | **INT. HARRY'S APT.(N)** <br> **CORRIDOR** <br><br> Scene 377 <br> 4/8 <br><br> Harry runs to his apt. <br> Passes Ron in hallway. | #1 - HARRY <br> #12 - RON <br> #14 - BOB | 700 LAGUNA STREET <br> #306, 307 <br><br> PROPS <br> Blue Pouch |

| DAY/DATE | SET/SCENES | CAST/ATMOS | STAGE/LOCATION |
|---|---|---|---|
| DAY 20 cont'd. | **INT. HARRY'S APT.(N)** | # 1 – HARRY | 700 LAGUNA STREET |
| | Scenes 378, 379 | #12 – RON (378) | #306, 307 |
| | 3 pages | #14 – BOB    " | PROPS |
| | | | Blue Pouch |
| | Harry goes into apt. Calls Mr. C., not in. They will call him back. Tells them they don't have his #. Neighbors are angry that he is owner. Harry kicks them out of his apt. -- no time to talk now. Phone rings. It is Mark telling Harry that Martin is no longer with firm and Harry should forget all. Mark will be watching. | | |
| | | END OF TWENTIETH DAY | |

151

| DAY/DATE | SET/SCENES | CAST/ATMOS | STAGE/LOCATION |
|---|---|---|---|
| DAY 21 FRIDAY 12/22/-- 3-2/8 | **EXT. PHONE BOOTH (D)** Scene 92 1-1/8th | # 1 - HARRY EXTRAS Gen St. Atmos | PROPS Blue Pouch Tapes inside. |
| | Harry calls Mr. C. for appt. to deliver pouch. Gets in and leaves. | | CONST. Telephone Booth Neon Sign |
| COMPANY MOVES TO 765 MISSION STREET | | | |

| DAY/DATE | SET/SCENES | CAST/ATMOS | STAGE/LOCATION |
|---|---|---|---|
| DAY 21 cont'd. | **INT. CATHOLIC CHURCH CONFESSIONAL (D)** | # 1 – HARRY | 765 MISSION ST. |
| | Scenes 230, 231 6/8 | EXTRAS Priest (o/s) Boy (14 yrs) Atmos-church | PROPS Blue Pouch |
| | Scene 230 (2/8) – Harry goes into church. | | |
| | Scene 231 (4/8) – Goes to confessional, tells all, but... | | NOTES Welfare Worker? |
| | **INT. LAUNDRY (D)** | # 1 – HARRY #27 – L/LADY #28 – L/L BOY | PROPS Harry's Laundry Money |
| | Scene 39 5/8 | EXTRAS Atmos. | Groceries Glass/water Dish towel |
| | Harry does trick, gets laundry & goes. | | NOTES Welfare worker |

153

| DAY/DATE | SET/SCENES | CAST/ATMOS | STAGE/LOCATION |
|---|---|---|---|
| DAY 21 cont'd. | INT. **AUD/SLIDES** | | |
| | Scenes 120 (part), 123, 125 | EXTRAS Woman/blue box | PROPS Blue box, car(nd) Diagrams |
| | Scene 120 (3/8) – Car speeding through city. | | NOTES Slides which will be used later in Convention Scene |
| | Scene 123 (2/8) – CU of blue box, and diagram of interference. | | |
| | Scene 125 (1/8) – Pretty woman installs blue box. | | |

END OF TWENTY-FIRST DAY – END OF FOURTH WEEK.

* * * * * CHRISTMAS & NEW YEAR'S BREAK * * * * *

# Shooting Schedule

| DAY/DATE | SET/SCENES | CAST/ATMOS | STAGE/LOCATION |
|---|---|---|---|
| DAY 22 WEDNESDAY 1/3/-- | **EXT. CONTINENTAL LODGE (D)** | # 1 - HARRY | 2550 VAN NESS CONTINENTAL VAGABOND MOTEL |
| 1-3/8 | Scenes 232, 233, 234 235, 236 | EXTRAS Gen. Atmos. | PROPS Attache case. |
|  | 5/8 |  |  |
|  | Harry goes to motel looks it over, and registers. |  |  |
|  | **INT. CONTINENTAL LOBBY (D)** | # 1 - HARRY #36 - CLERK | 2550 VAN NESS |
|  | Scene 237 3/8 |  | PROPS Attache case Motel Key Registration |
|  | Harry wants room B-7 but settles for room next door. |  |  |

155

| DAY/DATE | SET/SCENES | CAST/ATMOS | STAGE/LOCATION |
|---|---|---|---|
| DAY 22 cont'd. | **INT. CONTINENTAL CORRIDOR (D)**<br><br>Scene 238<br>2/8<br><br>Harry goes to his room. Room B-7 is definitely occupied. | #1 - HARRY | PROPS<br>Attache case<br>"Do not disturb"<br>sign - B-7<br>Room key. |
| | **INT. CONTINENTAL CORRIDOR (N)**<br><br>Scene 254<br>1/8th<br><br>Do Not Disturb sign is gone. Harry picks lock and goes in B-7. | #1 - HARRY | PROPS<br>Ring of lock picks |

END OF TWENTY-SECOND DAY

| DAY/DATE | SET/SCENES | CAST/ATMOS | STAGE/LOCATION |
|---|---|---|---|
| DAY 23 THURSDAY 1/4/-- | INT. MOTEL ROOM B-5 HARRY'S - (D) | # 1 - HARRY | 2550 VAN NESS CONTINENTAL LODGE |
| 2-6/8 | Scenes 239, 240, 241, 242, 243, 244, 245, 246, 247, 248, 249, 250. | | PROPS Attache Case Motel Key Jeweller's Drill "Bug" Elect. Box |
| | 2-3/8 | | CONSTRUCTION Putty & Matching touch-up paint in case Take 1 isn't a Print. |
| | Harry goes into room. Goes to window. POV B-7 with curtains drawn. Goes back. Puts bug under sink and hears violent sounds coming from B-7. Stops listening, turns on tv full blast. Hides in bed. | | |

| DAY/DATE | SET/SCENES | CAST/ATMOS | STAGE/LOCATION |
|---|---|---|---|
| DAY 23 cont'd. | **INT. MOTEL ROOM B-5** **HARRY'S - (N)** | # 1 - HARRY | PROPS Attache Case Motel Key |
| | Scenes 251, 252, 253. 3/8 | | |
| | Harry wakes up. Quiet next door. His TV still blaring. Harry goes to Room B-7 to look. | | |
| | END OF TWENTY-THIRD DAY | | |

| DAY/DATE | SET/SCENES | CAST/ATMOS | STAGE/LOCATION |
|---|---|---|---|
| DAY 24 FRIDAY 1/5/-- <br><br> 2-3/8ths | **INT. MOTEL ROOM B-7 (N)** <br><br> Scenes 255, 256, 257, 258, 259, 260. <br> 6/8ths <br><br> Room is straight. <br> No "body" in sight. <br> Harry checks all, goes into bathroom. | # 1 - HARRY | 2550 VAN NESS CONTINENTAL LODGE (INCL. PREVIOUS FOOTAGE) <br><br> PROPS <br> Lock Picks <br> Motel Ads <br> Sanitized glasses |

159

| DAY/DATE | SET/SCENES | CAST/ATMOS | STAGE/LOCATION |
|---|---|---|---|
| DAY 24 cont'd. | **INT. BATHROOM B-7 (N)** | #1 - HARRY | EFX Water in toilet becomes bloody. |
| | Scenes 261, 262, 263, 264, 265, 266, 267, 268, 270, 270. | | |
| | 1-3/8ths | | |
| | Bathroom is ok, but toilet won't stop running. Harry tries to stop it -- fills up with blood. And over flows. Harry is scared to death. He runs out of bathroom to get air. | | |

| DAY/DATE | SET/SCENES | CAST/ATMOS | STAGE/LOCATION |
|---|---|---|---|
| DAY 24 cont'd. | **INT. MOTEL ROOM & BATHROOM (repeat) (N)** | # 1 – HARRY | |
| | Scene 354 1/8th | | |
| | Harry tracks blood on tile and carpet. | | |
| | **EXT. MOTEL WINDOW B-7)** **(N)** | #1 – HARRY | |
| | Scene 269 1/8th | | |
| | POV Harry getting air at window. | | |

END OF TWENTY-FOURTH DAY – END OF FIFTH WEEK

| DAY/DATE | SET/SCENES | CAST/ATMOS | STAGE/LOCATION |
|---|---|---|---|
| DAY 25 MONDAY 1/8/-- | **INT. B-7 MOTEL ROOM & BATH (D)** | #2 - ANN #3 - MARK #4 - MR. C. | 2550 VAN NESS CONTINENTAL LODGE |
| 1-3/8 | Scenes 363, 359, 360, 361, 356 | | PROPS Plastic Sheet Bloody Tissues Short-bladed knives Blood |
| | 1-3/8 | | EFX Stab wounds on body. Blood. |
| | Scene 363 (2/8) - Mr. C. plays tape for Ann and Mark. Mark locks door. | | |
| | Scenes 359, 360, 361. (6/8) - Mr. C is killed with small knives. | | |
| | Scene 356 (3/8) - Bloody tissue in toilet. Mark cleans off walls. Mr. C on plastic sheet to catch drips. | | |

END OF TWENTY-FIFTH DAY

162

| DAY/DATE | SET/SCENES | CAST/ATMOS | STAGE/LOCATION |
|---|---|---|---|
| DAYS 26&27 TUESDAY 1/9/-- WEDNESDAY 1/10/-- 5-4/8 | **EXT/INT. BUS #1(D)** Scenes 284, 285, 289, 291. 4/8 | # 2 - ANN #37 - DRIVER BUS #1 #38-DRIVER #2 <u>EXTRAS</u> Passengers | CLAY ST., 6TH STREET FULTON <u>EFX</u> Fog? |
| | Sc. 284 - Bus in fog (1/8) | | |
| | Sc. 285 - Moving on Ann in bus. (1/8) | | |
| | Sc. 289 - Ext. Moving view on bus (on hill) (1/8). | | |
| | Sc. 291 - Moving View on Ann's bus. (1/8). | | |

| DAY/DATE | SET/SCENES | CAST/ATMOS | STAGE/LOCATION |
|---|---|---|---|
| | **INT. BUS #1 (D)** | #1 – HARRY | |
| | | #2 – ANN | |
| | Scenes 298, 300, 301, 302. | #38 – DRIVER | PROPS |
| | 1-3/8 | BUS #2 | Attache Case |
| | | EXTRAS | |
| | Sc. 298 (3/8) Harry gets on behind Ann. | Passengers | |
| | Scs. 300, 301, 302 (1 pg.) Harry talks to Ann. She moves away. He follows. | | |
| | **EXT. BUS #1 (LATE AFTERNOON** (D) | #1 – HARRY | |
| | | #2 – ANN | |
| | Scene 299 (1/8) Bus through thickening fog. | #38 – DRIVER #2 | PROPS |
| | | EXTRAS | Attache Case |
| | | Passengers | |

164

| DAY/DATE | SET/SCENES | CAST/ATMOS | STAGE/LOCATION |
|---|---|---|---|
| DAYS 26&27 cont'd. | EXT. BUS #1 (N) | #1 - HARRY<br>#2 - ANN<br>#37 - DRIVER #1 | PROPS<br>Attache Case |
| | Scs. 303, 304.<br>2/8 | | |
| | | EXTRAS<br>Passengers | |
| | Bus through night.<br>Ann tries to ignore<br>Harry who's behind her. | | |
| | INT. BUS #1 (N) | # 1 - HARRY<br># 2 - ANN<br>#37 - DRIVER<br>BUS #1 | CLAY STREET<br>6TH STREET<br>FULTON |
| | Scenes 305, 306<br>1-6/8 | | PROPS<br>Attache case |
| | | EXTRAS<br>Atmos on bus. | |
| | Harry talks to Ann<br>who isn't interested.<br>He repeats part of the<br>"Ann/Mark" tape -- she's<br>scared and runs. He<br>follows her. | | |

| DAY/DATE | SET/SCENES | CAST/ATMOS | STAGE/LOCATION |
|---|---|---|---|
| DAYS 26&27 cont'd. | **EXT. POLES & LINES (INSERTS)** (D) | | CLAY ST. SIXTH ST. FULTON ST. |
| | Scenes 286, 290, 294. 3/8. | | |
| | Scene 286 (1/8) Wires short. | | |
| | Scene 290 (1/8) Wires separate. | | |
| | Scene 294 (1/8) Antennae glide straight | | |
| | **EXT. STREET & HARRY'S BUS** (D) | #1 – HARRY #39 – DRIVER #2 | PROPS Attache Case |
| | Sc. 297 1/8 | EXTRAS Passengers | |
| | Harry gets off, falls down, goes to Ann's bus. Gets on. | STUNT DOUBLE? | |

END OF TWENTY-SIXTH AND TWENTY-SEVENTH DAYS.

166

*Shooting Schedule*

| DAY/DATE | SET/SCENES | CAST/ATMOS | STAGE/LOCATION |
|---|---|---|---|
| DAYS 26&27 cont'd. | **INT. BUS #2 & STREET** (D) | #1 – HARRY #38–DRIVER #2 | PROPS |
| | Scenes 287, 288, 292, 293, 295, 296. 7/8 | EXTRAS Passengers | |
| | Sc. 287. (1/8) Moving view on Harry. | | |
| | Sc. 288 (1/8) POV Bus #1 | | |
| | Sc. 292 (1/8) Bus #2 climbs hill. | | |
| | Sc. 293 (1/8) Harry watches Ann's bus. | | |
| | Sc. 295 (1/8) Moving view – Bus #2. | | |
| | Sc. 296 (2/8) Harry gets up, heads for Ann's bus. | | |

167

| DAY/DATE | SET/SCENES | CAST/ATMOS | STAGE/LOCATION |
|---|---|---|---|
| DAYS 26&27 cont'd. | EXT. BUS & STREET (N) | #1 - HARRY | PROPS |
| | Scenes 307, 308 | #2 - ANN | Attache Case |
| | 3/8 | #38 - DRIVER | |
| | | BUS #2 | EFX |
| | Ann runs onto stairs. Harry follows, trying to make her listen. | | Fog? |

| DAY/DATE | SET/SCENES | CAST/ATMOS | STAGE/LOCATION |
|---|---|---|---|
| DAY 28<br>THURSDAY<br>1/11/-- | EXT. STEPPED ST. (N)<br><br>Scenes 309, 310, 311,<br>312, 313, 314,<br>315, 316. | # 1 - HARRY<br># 2 - ANN | PROPS<br>Attache Case<br><br>EFX<br>Fog |
| 5-4/8 | 1-1/8 | | |
| | Harry says he's a good<br>person. Ann runs. | | |

| DAY/DATE | SET/SCENES | CAST/ATMOS | STAGE/LOCATION |
|---|---|---|---|
| | **EXT. PARK (N)** | # 1 - HARRY | PROPS |
| | | # 2 - ANN | Attache Case |
| | Scenes 317, 318, 319, | | |
| | 321, 322, 323, | | EFX |
| | 324, 325, 326, | | |
| | 327, 328, 329, | | |
| | 330, 331, 332. | | |
| | | | |
| | 4-3/8 | | |
| | | | |
| | Harry follows Ann into | | |
| | park & tells all. When | | |
| | he's done, she's gone. | | |
| | | | |
| | END OF TWENTY-EIGHTH DAY | | |

| DAY/DATE | SET/SCENES | CAST/ATMOS | STAGE/LOCATION |
|---|---|---|---|
| DAY 29<br>FRIDAY<br>1/12/--<br><br>2-7/8ths | INT. **HARRY'S RM (D)**<br><br>Scs. 380, 381, 382,<br>383, 384, 385,<br>386, 387, 388,<br>389, 390, 391,<br>392, 393, 394,<br>395, 396, 367/<br><br>Harry plays sax. Phone rings.<br>No one there. Becomes<br>paranoid. Takes phone apart--<br>nothing. Takes plates from<br>wall, moves chairs, rolls up<br>carpet, checks Madonna--<br>still nothing. Checks walls<br>for wires, peels paper, rips<br>up baseboard, floorboards,<br>Again...nothing. | #1 - HARRY | 700 LAGUNA ST.<br><br>PROPS<br>Saxophone<br>Records<br>Pencil Screw-<br>driver<br>Telephone,<br>Wall Switches<br>to take apart.<br>Knife to slit<br>sofa.<br>Bowl of hot<br>water.<br>Razor blade.<br>Screwdriver.<br>Sponge. |

END OF TWENTY-NINTH DAY

| DAY/DATE | SET/SCENES | CAST/ATMOS | STAGE/LOCATION |
|---|---|---|---|
| DAYS 30&31 MONDAY 1/15/-- | **EXT. HARRY'S WAREHOUSE (D)** <br> Scene 50 <br> 2/8 <br> Harry enters elev. | #1 - HARRY <br><br> EXTRAS <br> Warehouse Types | 255 KANSAS ST. <br><br> PROPS <br> Asst'd. Boxes <br><br> EFX <br> Practical elev. |
| TUESDAY 1/16/-- <br> 11-6/8 | **INT. WAREHOUSE (D)** <br><br> Scenes 51, 52, 53, <br> 54, 55, 56, <br> 57, 59, 60, <br> 61, 63, 65, <br> 67, 69, 70, <br> 72, 73, 74, <br> 75, 76, 77, <br> 78, 79, 80, <br> 82, 83, 84, <br> 85, 86, 88, <br> 89, 90, 91. | #1 - HARRY <br> #5 - STAN | PROPS <br> Tape <br> Tape Recorders <br> Magazines <br> Coffee & Pot <br> Filter Device <br> (Sc. 80) <br> Photo - Ann/Mark. |

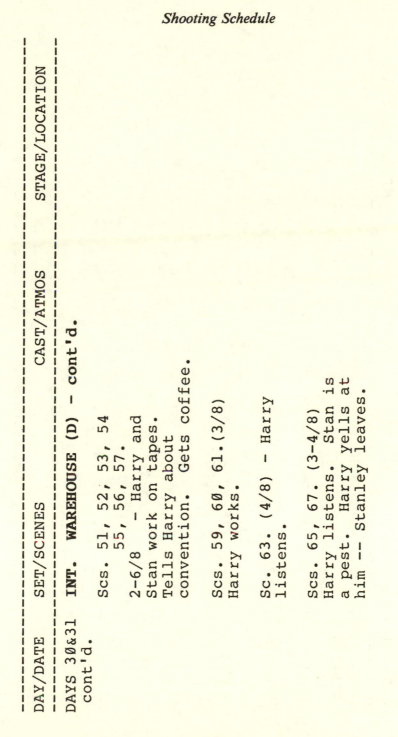

| DAY/DATE | SET/SCENES | CAST/ATMOS | STAGE/LOCATION |
|---|---|---|---|
| DAYS 30&31 cont'd. | **INT. WAREHOUSE (D) – cont'd.** | | |
| | Scs. 51, 52, 53, 54 55, 56, 57. 2-6/8  – Harry and Stan work on tapes. Tells Harry about convention. Gets coffee. | | |
| | Scs. 59, 60, 61.(3/8) Harry works. | | |
| | Sc. 63. (4/8) – Harry listens. | | |
| | Scs. 65, 67. (3-4/8) Harry listens. Stan is a pest. Harry yells at him -- Stanley leaves. | | |

173

| DAY/DATE | SET/SCENES | CAST/ATMOS | STAGE/LOCATION |
|---|---|---|---|
| DAYS 30&31 cont'd. | **INT. WAREHOUSE (D) – cont'd.** | | |
| | Scs. 69, 70. (4/8) Harry listens to tapes. | | |
| | Scs. 72, 73, 74, 75 76, 77, 78, 79, 80. (1-3/8) Harry listens. Adds a special filter. | | |
| | Scs. 82, 83, 84, 85, 86. (1 page) – Harry hears "kill us" and is upset. | | |
| | Scs. 88, 89, 90, 91. (4/8 ) Harry rewinds tape, looks at photo of Ann & Mark. | | |

END OF THIRTIETH AND THIRTY-FIRST DAYS

| DAY/DATE | SET/SCENES | CAST/ATMOS | STAGE/LOCATION |
| --- | --- | --- | --- |
| DAYS 32, 33, 34 | INT. **WAREHOUSE (N)** | | 255 KANSAS ST. |
| WEDNESDAY 1/17/-- | Scs. 160, 161, 162, 163, 164, 165, 166, 167, 168, 169, 170, 171, 172, 173. | # 1 – HARRY<br># 5 – STAN<br># 6 – PAUL<br># 8 – MORAN<br># 9 – MEREDITH<br>#10 – MILLARD<br>#17 – LURLEEN | PROPS<br>4 bottles whisky<br>ice<br>sack beer cans<br>bag potato chips<br>cups f/drinks<br>record player<br>records<br>Mark/Ann tape (to (play)<br>Name tags<br>O/N bag<br>Pen (Moran's ad) |
| THURSDAY 1/18/-- | 19-4/8 | | |
| FRIDAY 1/19/-- | 19-4/8 | | |

All arrive, have party. Harry & Meredith dance. Paul cuts in. Moran tells about welfare fund. Harry tells him about bugged bait

continued...

175

| DAY/DATE | SET/SCENES | CAST/ATMOS | STAGE/LOCATION |
|---|---|---|---|
| DAYS 32, 33, 34 | **INT. WAREHOUSE (N) - cont'd.** <br><br> tank. Mark/Ann tape plays. Harry upset. Harry talks about current surveillance problem. Won't let Moran see any of his stuff. Moran plays back "Harry/Meredith" tape. Embarrassed and upset he kicks them all out. Meredith stays. | | Bookshelf w/radios, ashtrays, packs of cigarettes, cigar humidors, vases, etc. <br> Bouquet w/mike <br> Cig. pack - elect. components <br> Blackboard/chalk <br> Cassette recorder (Moran) <br> Cot & Blanket <br><br> <u>EFX</u> <br> Light change |

END OF THIRTY-SECOND, THIRTY-THIRD AND THIRTY-FOURTH DAYS

END OF SEVENTH WEEK

| DAY/DATE | SET/SCENES | CAST/ATMOS | STAGE/LOCATION |
|---|---|---|---|
| DAYS 35&36 | INT. WAREHOUSE (N) | # 1 – HARRY<br># 9 –MEREDITH | 255 KANSAS ST. |
| MONDAY 1/22/–– | Scs. 174, 175, 176, 177, 178, 179 180, 181, 183, 184. | | PROPS<br>4 bottles whisky<br>ice<br>sack beer cans<br>bag potato chips<br>cups f/drinks<br>record player<br>records<br>Mark/Ann tape<br>(to play)<br>Name tags<br>O/N bag<br>Pen (Moran's ad)<br>Bookshelf<br>w/radios,<br>ashtrays, packs<br>of cigarettes,<br>cigar humidors,<br>vases, etc.<br>Bouquet w/mike |
| TUESDAY 1/23/–– | 10-1/8 | | |
| 10-6/8 | Meredith and Harry talk about his work. He replays Ann/Mark tape. Harry listens. Meredith undresses, then undresses Harry. He is not interested. Meredith persists. He gives in. They fall asleep on sofa. Harry dreams and sleeps . | | |

| DAY/DATE | SET/SCENES | CAST/ATMOS | STAGE/LOCATION |
|---|---|---|---|
| DAYS 35&36 cont'd. | INT. **WAREHOUSE (N) – cont'd.** | | PROPS – cont'd. <br> Cig. pack – elect. components <br> Blackboard/chalk <br> Cassette recorder (Moran) <br> Cot & Blanket <br><br> EFX <br> Light change |
| | INT. **WAREHOUSE (N)** #1 – HARRY <br><br> Scs. 186, 187. <br> 5/8 <br><br> Harry wakes up. Meredith gone, phone humming. | | PROPS <br> Phone <br> Cot & Blanket |

END OF THIRTY-FIFTH AND THIRTY-SIXTH DAYS

| DAY/DATE | SET/SCENES | CAST/ATMOS | STAGE/LOCATION |
|---|---|---|---|
| DAY 37 | INT. WAREHOUSE (N) | #1 - HARRY | 255 KANSAS STREET |
| WEDNESDAY 1/24/-- | Scenes 337, 338, 339, 340, 341, 342, 343, 344, 345, 346, 347, 348, 349, 350, 351, 352, 353, 355, 357, 358, 362, 364. | | PROPS<br>Attache Case<br>Beer Can<br><br>EFX<br>Light Change<br>(Off/On) |
| 5-1/8 | | | |
| 4-6/8 | | | |

Scs. 337 thru 353 - Harry creeps upstairs. Kicks beer can, is startled. Lights go out. He continues. Turns lights back on. Hears Mark/Ann tape playing. Sees everything has been searched. Goes to window. Sees two men running away. Plays tapes again -- discovers new information. (3-6/8)

179

| DAY/DATE | SET/SCENES | CAST/ATMOS | STAGE/LOCATION |
|---|---|---|---|
| DAY 37 cont'd. | **INT.  WAREHOUSE (N) – cont'd.** | | |
| | Sc. 355 – Harry remembers bloody shoes. (2/8) | | |
| | Scs. 357, 358 – Harry listens to tape (3/8) | | |
| | Sc. 362 – Harry sees it all (1/8) | | |
| | Sc. 364 – Shuts off recorder. (1/8). | | |

| DAY/DATE | SET/SCENES | CAST/ATMOS | STAGE/LOCATION |
|---|---|---|---|
| DAY 37 cont'd. | **EXT. WAREHOUSE ALLEY** **(N)** | #1 – HARRY | PROPS Attache Case |
| | Scenes 333, 334, 335, 336. | | |
| | 4/8 | | |
| | Harry sees lights on in warehouse. Goes to see what is going. Uses stairs -- not elevator. | | |

END OF THIRTY-SEVENTH DAY

| DAY/DATE | SET/SCENES | CAST/ATMOS | STAGE/LOCATION |
|---|---|---|---|
| DAY 38 | **INT.  CAR(TRAVELING) (N)** | # 1-HARRY | PROPS |
| THURSDAY 1/25/-- | Scenes 144, 146, 147, 148, 149, 151, 152, 153, 155, 157, 158, 159. | # 5-STAN | Sedan (Paul) |
| | | # 6-PAUL | Mustang (Willie) |
| | | # 8-MORAN | License as |
| | | # 9-MEREDITH | desc. or as/is. |
| | | #10-MILLARD | Radio in sedan |
| | | #17-LURLEEN | |
| | | #35-WILLIE/YNG DRIVER | |
| 3 pages | 2-4/8 | STUNT.DBL FOR WILLIE | VEHICLES |
| | | | Staff Car (Sedan) |
| | | | Mustang |

Sc. 144 – Introductions as Mustang passes Paul. Paul tails them. (4/8)

Sc. 146 – Paul pulls up next to Mustang (2/8)

Scs. 147, 148 – Field car? (2/8)

continued...

182

| DAY/DATE | SET/SCENES | CAST/ATMOS | STAGE/LOCATION |
|---|---|---|---|
| DAY 38 | **INT. CAR (TRAVELING) - cont'd. (N)** | | |
| | Sc. 149 - Lurlee wants them to stop. Paul #1 Tail Man and can't. (3/8). | | |
| | Scs. 151, 152, 153, 155 - Stan says Paul is "Bullitt". Paul checks out license plate. (6/8) | | |
| | Scs. 157, 158. Meredith is bugged. Paul calls Mustang driver by name, "WILLIE" (2/8) | | |
| | Sc. 159 - Staff car pulls away from Willie who is amazed. (1/8) | | |

183

| DAY/DATE | SET/SCENES | CAST/ATMOS | STAGE/LOCATION | PROPS |
|---|---|---|---|---|
| DAY 38 cont'd. | **EXT. STREET – SEDAN AND MUSTANG (N)**<br><br>Scenes 145, 150, 154, 156.<br><br>4/8<br><br>Sc. 145 – Paul chases Mustang (1/8)<br><br>Sc. 150 – Mustang careens around corner – almost out of control. (1/8)<br><br>Sc. 154 – CU – Mustang's license plates. (1/8)<br><br>Sc. 156 – Paul pulls up next to Mustang at light. (1/8) | # 1–HARRY<br># 5–STAN<br># 6–PAUL<br># 8–MORAN<br># 9–MEREDITH<br>#10–MILLARD<br>#17–LURLEEN<br>#35–WILLIE/YNG DRIVER<br>STUNT DOUBLE/WILLIE | | |

END OF THIRTY-EIGHTH DAY

| DAY/DATE | SET/SCENES | CAST/ATMOS | STAGE/LOCATION |
|---|---|---|---|
| DAY 39<br><br>FRIDAY<br>1/26/--<br><br>6-6/8 | INT. CONVENTION BAR (N)<br><br>Scenes 133 - 136.<br>1-5/8<br><br>Harry makes phone call. Disconnected number. Accosted by Mr. C's assistant (Martin). Told to bring pouch on Sunday. Martin asks what's on tapes. Harry ignores him, and goes back to convention. | # 1 - HARRY<br>#7 - MARTIN | ST. FRANCIS HOTEL GRAND BALLROOM<br><br>PROPS<br>Pay Phone<br>Liquor for people<br>    at bar.<br>Draft beer for<br>    Martin. |

185

| DAY/DATE | SET/SCENES | CAST/ATMOS | STAGE/LOCATION |
|---|---|---|---|
| DAY 39 cont'd. | INT. CONVENTION BOOTH AREA (N)  Scenes 137, 138, 139, 140, 141, 142.  4-3/8  Paul grabs Harry. Takes him to Moran. They've bugged the Ladies' Room. They listen. Stan on guard at door with walkie-talkie. Woman exits. Then Meredith. They're joined by Bill and Lurleen. They leave for Harry's warehouse. | # 1-HARRY # 6-PAUL # 5-STAN # 9-MEREDITH # 7-MARTIN #10-MILLARD #17-LURLEEN # 8 MORAN IN B/R #43 1ST WOMAN IN B/R  EXTRAS 125 mixed business types men & women. | PROPS Walkie-Talkie Loudspeaker O/Night case— Meredith. |

| DAY/DATE | SET/SCENES | CAST/ATMOS | STAGE/LOCATION |
|---|---|---|---|
| DAY 39 cont'd. | **<u>EXT. PARKING LOT (N)</u>**<br><br>Scene 143. (6/8)<br><br>They all get into Paul's car and leave. | # 1-HARRY<br># 5-STAN<br># 6-PAUL<br># 8-MORAN<br>#10-MILLARD<br>#17-LURLEEN<br># 9-MEREDITH<br><br><u>EXTRAS</u><br>Pkg Attdnt.<br>Atmos as needed. | <u>PROPS</u><br>Grey sedan w/ official seal. |

END OF THIRTY-NINTH DAY

END OF EIGHTH WEEK

| DAY/DATE | SET/SCENES | CAST/ATMOS | STAGE/LOCATION |
|---|---|---|---|
| DAY 40<br><br>MONDAY<br>1/29/--<br><br>4 pages | **INT. CONVENTION**<br>**LOBBY/BOOTH AREA**<br><br>Scenes 109, 110, 111,<br>112, 113, 114,<br>115, 116, 117,<br>119.<br><br>2-3/8<br><br>Harry goes into<br>convention. Gets name<br>tag. Views display, moves<br>toward auditorium.<br><br>Scene 118 (1/8) - Harry's<br>POV of Martin in crowd. | #1-HARRY<br>#34-MAN/BOOTH<br>#7-MARTIN<br><br>EXTRAS<br>Hostesses<br>Conventioneers | ST. FRANCIS HOTEL<br>GRAND BALLROOM<br><br>PROPS<br>White name cards.<br>Components "L-T<br>500.<br>Drinks.<br>Name card --<br>"HARRY CAUL" |

188

| DAY/DATE | SET/SCENES | CAST/ATMOS | STAGE/LOCATION |
|---|---|---|---|
| DAY 40 cont'd. | **INT. CONVENTION AUDITORIUM (N)**<br><br>Scenes 120(part),121, 122, 123, 124.<br><br>1-5/8<br><br>Harry goes into slide show. Paul spots him. Takes him off for a drink. | # 1-HARRY<br># 6-PAUL<br>#33-SPEAKER<br><br>EXTRAS<br>Audience | PROPS<br>Name Cards<br>Paper/Speaker<br>Slides as desc.<br>Flyers is bags.<br><br>NOTE - page<br>Credit for 121<br>taken on Day 21. |

END OF FORTIETH DAY

| DAY/DATE | SET/SCENES | CAST/ATMOS | STAGE/LOCATION |
|---|---|---|---|
| DAY 41 | INT. CONVENTION BOOTH AREA (N) | # 1-HARRY<br># 6-PAUL<br>#5-STAN | ST. FRANCIS HOTEL (MAIN BALLROOM) |
| TUESDAY 1/30/--<br>8-7/8 | Scenes 126, 127, 128.<br>8-7/8 | # 8-MORAN<br># 9-MEREDITH<br>#45 MAN IN<br># BOOTH #2 | PROPS<br>Name tags<br>Fly sheets<br>Pillow<br>Cigarettes<br>Drinks<br>Red Telephone<br>Moran S-15 bug<br>Harmonica<br>Sign: "BOOTH 34 WILLIAM P. MORAN & ASSOCIATES." |
| | Harry and Paul go to Moran's booth and see S-15 demo. Dialogue w/Stan. He goes. Harry talks w/bystander and demo man. Harry won't endorse product. He leaves. | | |

END OF FORTY-FIRST DAY

END OF NINTH WEEK...END OF SHOW!!

190

# X
## FINAL COMMENTS

After many days of hard work, your production board is now fully laid out. You have calculated that it will take 41 days to shoot the scripted material, including two weeks of Second Camera work which was scheduled to be done with the First Camera work. This gives you the opportunity to have greater coverage of the material which is scheduled for the first two working weeks.

You have now gone through THE CONVERSATION. You have broken down and scheduled one of the more complicated scripts and will be ready now to learn how to turn all this information into a budget. That is covered fully in *Film Budgeting*.

Here are a few more hints which might help you on your next (or first) feature project.

1)   After finishing your breakdown, go over each day's schedule with the director and see if he agrees with it. It is important that the director be enthusiastic about your schedule and believe that he can shoot it. He should understand it and believe that it is realistically laid out. Going over the board very carefully with the director will

give you the opportunity to understand how he thinks. The more you understand the way the director thinks, the more accurately you will be able to lay out your schedule. Remember, you are scheduling the show in the best way the director can shoot it—not the best way that *you* would shoot it.

2)    Understand that a director may want to add a scene or expand a scene (or drop scenes). As the creative force on the picture, he has that privilege and you must be flexible enough to be able to deal with it. Your schedule must be able to be re-arranged or altered if and when the need arises. If you feel that the suggested change will add more than reasonable costs to the picture, then you should make the director and the producer aware in a diplomatic way.

3)    The question, "what if . . .?" will haunt you every day on a production. A production manager's role is flexible. He must constantly be building alternate routes for each and every day. As a type of Line Quarterback for the producer and/or studio, it is his responsibility to keep the film moving along on a straight course.

If a film company stops shooting or is delayed in any way, the flow of dollars does not necessarily stop. If the production is not gaining ground each day towards completing pages of the script, then massive losses are as certain as getting your feet wet from the massive tidal wave you are watching.

4)    Communication is so essential that it cannot be over-stressed. A production manager is middle management—the link between the production and those who are responsible for the total costs of the project. If the production manager maintains a solid and open communication sys-

tem with both sides, he will be far ahead of the game in problem-solving and, therefore, on the way to a more smoothly run production.

5)   Keep organized. One way we have found is to keep your breakdown sheets with you at all times. They were your first contact with the script and, quite possibly, will be your most complete notes. Before you start shooting, we have found that it is a good idea to re-arrange them into the order of the production schedule, marking them with dividers. If your copy machine reduces, then you can reduce everything. It makes it much easier to carry it around. Include a map to the location for every scene and list the people to contact about that location. Also include a separate section with your cast and crew list, contact sheet, location list, etc. A good supply of note paper inserted into your book will be invaluable. Tape two or three pens inside the cover, and make sure you have a good supply of dimes for calling the production office. Rarely do locations have telephones which you may use. Most likely, you will find yourself on a street corner using the local public telephone. This book will be your production Bible—your ready reference to any question which may come up. Keep it up-to-date. If a scene changes, do a new breakdown sheet and put it in its proper place.

As you do more script breakdowns, you will find that the work goes more quickly. Playing the various roles of producer, director, actor, stunt coordinator, special effects coordinator, etc., can be a lot of fun.

GOOD LUCK! I'd love to hear from you and of your successes in production.

Let's make movies!!!

# GLOSSARY

**Note:** Words in *italics* are defined elsewhere in the glossary.

**Actors**
Those people who perform the action and say the dialogue as written in the screenplay according to the directions of the director. The main union/guild for actors is the Screen Actors Guild. See *S.A.G.*

**Added Scene**
When an additional scene needs to be inserted into a script which has already been numbered, instead of re-numbering all the following scenes, a letter is added, e.g., Scene 23-A.

**Animals**
When used in motion picture filming, animals require special handling, handlers, trainers, wranglers, etc. Many times, look-a-like animals will be used if the scene requires special tricks or actions.

**Art Department**
The department of a motion picture crew which is responsible for creating the "look" of a film. Staff usually includes an Art Director and/or Production Designer, Assistant Art Director & Draftsperson.

**Asterisk**
Used to indicate make-up and hair references when breaking down a script.

**Atmosphere**
See *extras.*

**Atmosphere Cars**
Any car, truck, motorcycle, etc., which is used in a scene on the production and is not used by the *principal players* or any of the *speaking parts.*

**Auditors**
That person assigned to account for the money spent on the production. (aka, Location Auditors, Production Accountants.)

**Bits**
(see *silents*)

**Breakdown**
(aka Script Breakdown) When prepared by the UPM or First A.D., it is a detailed analysis of each and every element needed to shoot a motion picture. Script Supervisors also prepare breakdowns, but for timing purposes.

**Breakdown Sheet**
A form used in breaking down the script into its individual elements, color-coded as follows: Day Exterior-Yellow, Night Exterior-Green, Day Interior-White and Night Exterior-Blue. See *Chapter Four.*

**Budget Form**
A detailed form which lists all the elements needed to make a film, the amount of time they will be needed and how much they will cost.

**Camera Car**
A specially-designed vehicle which holds the camera, its operator and usually the Director and Camera Assistant to film a travelling vehicle, person or to get *running shots* or *run-bys.*

**Camera Mount Car**
A special mount which allows the camera to be attached to an automobile for the purposes of filming the action either inside the car, or as the car is moving. (See also *camera car, front car mounts, side car mounts*).

**Camera Operator/Helicopter**
Sometimes, it is necessary to hire a special camera operator who is specially trained in filming motion pictures from helicopters. He will work closely with the helicopter pilot to get all necessary shots.

**Cast**
The performers appearing in a production. On a budget form, "Cast" refers specifically to all the actors, but not the *extras.*

**Character**
The name of the person an actor portrays in the production.

**Child Actors**
Any actor under the age of 18. There are strict rules governing the working hours/conditions, etc., of Child Actors. Usually, a teacher or welfare worker will be required. Check with *S.A.G.* for latest rules.

**Circle**
Used to indicate wardrobe when breaking down a script.

**Close**
Camera's POV will be in very close to the subject matter. Also see *close-up.*

**Close-up**
A shot of an actor in which you see mainly his head and shoulders.

**Color-Coding**
A system for simplifying the breakdown process. The first color code system is for the *breakdown sheets* themselves, and the second for the individual categories on the *breakdown sheets*. See Chapter Four.

**Completion Bond Company**
A company which, for a contracted fee usually based on a percentage of the budget, agrees to step in and pay the costs necessary to complete the production in the event the production goes over budget. It is customary for the completion bond company to then step in and closely oversee the production until it is finished.

**Copter Mount**
A special platform on a helicopter which holds the camera, e.g. Tyler Mount.

**Cover Set**
In the event of a sudden change of plans (actor is sick, weather is wrong for the exterior planned, etc.) this is an easily controllable, and sometimes moveable, set which can be shot without losing a day's work.

**Coverage**
All the shots necessary from all angles and *set-ups*. For example, if two actors are talking to each other, the director will want a *master shot* and coverage of the actors talking and listening to each other.

**Crane**
(aka Whirly) A large wheeled support which carries the camera on an arm which pivots. There are places for the director,

camera operator, and camera assistant to sit, and a trolley for the boom.

**Crew**
The term used to refer to all the technical and production people who work behind the camera to make a motion picture or television show.

**Cut To**
A phrase used to indicate that one scene should end and the next begin abruptly without the use of an *optical effect* such as a *fade, dissolve,* etc.

**C.Y.A.**
Cover Your Ass. One of the three Basic Rules. See Chapter Two.

**Dailies**
(aka Rushes) The scenes which were shot the previous shooting day and then screened for the producer, director, editor and others.

**Dawn**
It is important that "Dawn" and not "Day" be indicated on the breakdown sheet (shooting schedule, script, etc.) to indicate the specific of the action, as it implies a certain look (long shadows, pale light, etc.)

**Day**
What should be marked in the appropriate place on the breakdown sheet (shooting schedule, script, etc.) to indicate the time of day of the action. On the production strips, it is abbreviated, 'D'.

**Day Players**
The actors in the film who may have only a few lines or a few scenes. They are underlined in red in the script and noted in the "Cast - Speaking" box on breakdown sheets.

**Day Shots**
Those scenes in the production which are to be shot in daylight
—either real or artifical, interior or exterior.

**Day-For-Day**
Shooting Day scenes during actual daylight hours.

**Day-For-Night**
Although night interiors can usually be shot during the day by
dressing the windows, night exterior filming during the day
requires special filters to make it appear as if the scenes were
shot at night.

**Deleted Scene**
When a scene needs to be deleted from a script which has
already been numbered, instead of re-numbering all the following scenes, simply mark, "Scene 24 - Omitted."

**Director**
Hired by the producer, the director is the person responsible for
all the creative aspects of a motion picture or television show.

**Director of Photography**
The person responsible for the lights on the set and photography of the project, under the supervision of the director.

**Dissolve**
An optical effect which makes it seem as if one scene is literally
dissolving into the next scene. See also *Optical Effect.*

**Dolly**
A wheeled platform which holds the camera and its operator
for moving shots. Various kinds are: Western, Crab, Elemac,
etc.

**Double Move**
A move away from a location, and then back to it. Generally,
this is an expensive way of shooting and should be avoided.
There are exceptions: See Chapter Seven.

**Dress**
To change the appearance of an item so that it can be used on the set. For example, "dress the windows for night" means to change the look of the windows so that it will appear to be nighttime outside.

**Drop-and-Pick-Up**
When there are at least 10 free days between the day an actor last works and the next day he works on the same show, he may be dropped off salary and picked up again later. Can only be done once per show per actor.

**Dummy**
A life-size doll used to double a real actor in an extremely dangerous, or potentially dangerous, scene.

**Dusk**
It is important that 'Dusk' and not 'Night' be indicated on the breakdown sheet (shooting schedule, script, etc.) to indicate the specific of the action, as it implies a certain look (long shadows, warm light, etc.)

**DOP**
English and Australian abbreviation for Director of Photography.

**DP**
Abbreviation for Director of Photography.

**Establishing Shot**
Usually a long or full shot which identifies the location and sets the mood for the other shots.

**Executive Producer**
Generally refers to the person, or company, who has provided the financial resources for the production, although the title can be given for various other reasons to other people on the production.

**Extras**
Background atmosphere actors. Some extras are members of the *Screen Extras Guild*. In New York, they are members of *Screen Actors Guild*.

**Fade In**
The phrase used in a script at the beginning of a sequence to indicate that the scene should emerge from total darkness. See also *fade out.*

**Fade Out**
The phrase used in a script at the end of a sequence to indicate that the scene should disappear into total darkness. (aka Fade To Black).

**Financiers**
Those people/companies who put up the money necessary to make the motion picture or television project.

**First Unit**
The main shooting crew for a project, as opposed to Second Unit.

**Forced Call**
When an actor/crew member is brought back to work before having the minimum amount of time-off, and is paid a "forced call penalty payment."

**Front Car Mounts**
Special camera mounts which are placed on the front of the car. See *camera mounts.*

**Gaffer**
The chief electrician on the set who is responsible for setting the lights according to the instructions of the director of photography. The gaffer supervises his electrical crews' positioning of lights.

**Gofer**
(aka P.A. or Production Assistant). A slang term for a person on a production who does errands for (goes for) the producer, director, production manager, etc. Many production executives have begun their careers as gofers.

**Head Board**
(aka Header) The first strip on the production board. It is usually about 4 inches wide and contains all the information particular to a show. See Chapter Five.

**Helicopter Pilot/Special**
To fly, a helicopter with a camera mounts takes a helicopter pilot specially trained in motion picture filming, who will be able to work with the *camera operator* to get the necessary shots quickly and expertly.

**Helicopter With A Camera Mount**
A helicopter that has a special platform for the camera, e.g., Tyler Mount (aka 'Copter mount).

**High Angle**
Camera's POV for shooting will be elevated. Usually this notation implies that a crane will be used. See also *crane*.

**High Full Shot**
Generally implying a crane shot with the subject matter in the center of the frame and a good deal of foreground and background.

**Holding Board**
A two-panel board used when marking the strips. It is generally advisable to complete all strips for a scene/sequence before moving them from the holding board to the *production board*.

## Holding Days
The days when an actor is not required to be on-camera, but still has some other filming left to complete. See also *drop-and-pick up*.

## In-Town Picture
Usually refers to Los Angeles or New York, where home-based crews will not have to travel "to Location." Schedules are generally five-day work weeks. See also *location picture*.

## Independent Producer
Generally, it refers to a producer or production company who is not tied to a major studio for financing.

## Insert
A shot which is done earlier or later (sometimes by Second Unit) and then "inserted" into the film in the editing period.

## Insurance Company
The company (or companies) who have agreed to provide the multitudinous types of insurance coverage necessary when making a feature or television project.

## Location Manager
That person on the production staff responsible for finding and securing all the necessary locations which will be used in the production. Depending on the city, these people may be members of the *D.G.A.* or *I.A.T.S.E.*

## Location Picture
When the *cast* and *crew* have to travel away from the production company's home based. Schedules are generally six-day work weeks, and salaries are higher. Most times per diems/expenses are paid.

## Main Titles
Generally the front credits at the beginning of a film.

**Make-Up**
Any reference to make-up for the actors which is mentioned in the screenplay. When doing a breakdown, it should be marked with an asterisk and noted in its appropriate column.

**Master Shot**
The main shot of the entire action. See also *coverage.*

**Matching**
When editing, if care and attention to detail has not been paid to make sure that all make-up, hair, weather conditions, costumes, camera angles are in continuity, it will be jarring to the viewer as it doesn't match.

**Meal Penalty**
When actors and/or crew work more than the prescribed number of hours without having time-off for a meal, they are paid a penalty payment called a "meal penalty."

**Medium Shot**
A shot of the subject matter so that its entire image is clearly seen and not cut up, as in a *close shot,* or with a lot of foreground or background, as in a Long Shot.

**Moving View**
A shot which requires action, but generally implies a dolly—not a *camera car.*

**Night**
What should be marked in the appropriate place on the breakdown sheet (shooting schedule, script, etc.) to indicate the time of day of the action. On the production strips, it is abbreviated, 'N'.

**Night Shots**
Those scenes in the production which are to be shot at night —either interior or exterior. Unless it is necessary to show the

windows of the interior, most Night Interiors are scheduled to be shot *day-for-night.*

### Night-For-Night
When it is not possible to shoot *day-for-night,* then night exteriors (and certain night interiors) will be shot Night-For-Night.

### Off-Camera
Any action or dialogue which is not seen by the camera, but is heard by the audience.

### On-Camera
Any action which is seen by the camera.

### Optical Effect
Any effect which is added by the lab, such as a *fade, dissolve, wipe,* etc.

### Out-Of-Sequence
Usually, for expedience sake and budgetary reasons, motion pictures are not shot in chronological order. Scenes are arranged according to the 14 *parameter factors.* See Chapter Six.

### Over-The-Shoulder Shot
A shot appearing to be taken from "over the shoulder" of one actor when talking to another. Also see *coverage.*

### Page Count
When preparing breakdown sheets, the script is divided into eighths—the smallest allowable portion being one-eighth. Scene length is referred to in x-number of eighths.

### Panel
When describing the length of a Production Board, it is usually referred to by the number of panels, each panel being 10 wide and either 15 or 18-¼ inches high. THE CONVERSATION requires at least 8 panels.

**Parameter Guides**
(aka Parameter Factors) A set of 14 points to be considered, in order, when arranging and re-arranging the strips on the *production board* so as to arrive at the most efficient and cost-effective schedule. See Chapter Six.

**Penalty**
When certain union/guild rules are violated—intentionally or unintentionally—an additional sum of money will be paid to the person. The most usual penalties are *forced calls* and *meal penalties.*

**Period Piece**
When the time period of a screenplay is not present day, it is said to be a "period piece."

**Photo Double**
See *stunt photo double.*

**Picture Cars**
Any car, truck, motorcycle, etc., which is used in a scene on the production.

**Plays**
To appear, or to look on camera. "Let's see how this scene plays" means that the director wants to see how that particular scene looks. On a *production board,* it means "to be scheduled."

**Practical**
Anything on a set which actually works, e.g. *practical sink.*

**Practical Sink**
One which actually works on a set.

**Pre-Recorded**
To record any sort of music/effects/dialogue before it is actually filmed. Generally done in pre-production.

**Pre-Light**
Work done in advance by the electrical department, such as replacing the flourescent bulbs, before the crew comes in to shoot.

**Pre-Rig**
Work done in advance, such as putting up scaffolding, ceiling mounts, etc., before the crew comes in to shoot.

**Primary Locations**
The main or extremely special locations in a film. For example, "Union Square" is a primary location whereas 'McNaught's Office" is a *secondary location.*

**Principal Photography**
That portion of time scheduled to shoot all the scenes in the project. Sometimes, due to certain restrictions (weather, etc.) Second Unit is scheduled before commencement or after completion of principal photography.

**Principal Players**
The leads in the film, e.g., Harry Caul, Ann and Mark are considered Principals. They are underlined in red in the script and noted in the "Cast - Speaking" box on *breakdown sheets.*

**Process Shots**
A shot taken against a moving or still background of previously shot footage which is projected onto a transparent screen behind the current action which is being filmed.

**Producer**
The person exercising overall control over the production of a motion picture (or television show) and ultimately responsible for the show's success or failure.

**Production Manager**
The producer's executive assigned to the production, responsible for coordinating and supervising all administrative and

technical details of the production, and overseeing the activities of the entire crew.

**Production Notes**
That space on the breakdown sheet reserved for special notations such as, "technical advisor," "interpreter," "Christmas-time setting," etc.

**Production Strip Board**
The scheduling tool used by Production Managers and First A.D.'s to determine exactly how long it will take to shoot the production. Scene information is marked on strips which are then arranged and rearranged so that they show the most efficient and cost effective way to shoot the picture. The colors of the strips correspond to the Breakdown Sheets.

**Production Strips**
Made of cardboard, strips are either 15 or 18-1/4 inches long and fit into panels of a Production Strip Board. The strips are color-coded to match the *breakdown sheets.* See Chapter Five.

**Prop**
Short for Property—any portable object which is used in a scene by one of the actors.

**Property Department**
That department which is responsible for the manufacturer and/or purchase of all props used on the production.

**Re-Dress**
To change the look of a location or set. See *dress.*

**Run-Bys**
A travelling shot which differs from a *running shot* in that the subject matter travels past a stationary camera.

**Run-Of-Show-Deal**
A deal made for the services—usually of an actor/actress—for a specific salary for a specific number of weeks, no matter how many days the actor/actress works during that time.

**Running Shot**
A moving shot in which the camera travels at the same pace as the moving subject—person, car, etc., or is attached to the moving subject. Many times a hand-held camera is used for running shots of actors.

**S.A.G.**
Abbreviation for Screen Actors Guild, the collective bargaining union for actors who work in film (as opposed to videotape).

**Scene Name**
The identifier which describes the location of the action of the scene, e.g., "Union Square".

**Script Breakdown**
See *breakdown.*

**Second Assistant Director**
A DGA designated position on the crew who reports to the *first A.D.* and the *production manager* and is generally responsible for all the *cast* and *extras.* Can be up-graded on *second unit* to *first A.D.*

**Second Camera**
An additional camera used to film additional sequences at the same time as the *first camera.* a second camera is generally used in scenes which are difficult to re-stage.

**Second Unit**
A separate filming unit which shoots scenes generally not involving principal players. Although Second Unit can be shot during *principal photography,* it is not unusual for it to be shot either before or after.

## Second Unit D.P.

A cameraman who is hired to direct the photography of scenes which have fallen into the second unit listing. Shots which the first unit does not have time to complete, shots which are very complicated or require special skills or equipment (e.g., underwater scenes), or shots which are at a distant location are all examples of when a Second Unit Director of Photography could be hired. Many times, the First Unit Camera Operator and Assistant Cameraman are *up-graded* and moved to Second Unit for the necessary shots.

## Secondary Locations

As with *principal players,* and *supporting actors,* there are locations which are deemed more important—*primary locations*—than others, Secondary Locations.

## S.E.G.

Abbreviation for Screen Extras Guild, the collective bargaining union for *extras* who work in film (as opposed to video tape).

## Sequence

Any grouping of scenes which occur in the same location with the same theme, e.g., "Harry's Warehouse Sequence," "Union Square Opening Sequence," "Surveillance Sequence," etc.

## Set Dressing

Any item which is used in the decor of the set, and is not a prop. See also *prop*.

## Set-Up

The placement of the camera for a shot. Each time the camera is moved is another "set-up."

## Shooting Schedule

A detailed list of everyone and everything needed to shoot a particular scene. Compiled from information on the *breakdown sheets* and the *production board,* it is arranged in shooting order. See Chapter Nine.

**Side Car Mounts**
Special camera mounts which are placed on the sides of the car. See *camera mounts.*

**Silent Bits**
See *silents.*

**Silents**
An actor who performs an action in a scene which in some way affects either the direction of the story or the *principal players* in the scene is a Silent; e.g., a waiter who spills soup on the lead.

**Singles**
When shooting *coverage* of a scene, a director will want to get *close-up* shots of each actor, talking and listening. These close-ups are called "Singles."

**Slow Motion**
An effect achieved by running the film through the camera at a faster than normal speed (or through a projector, slower than normal.) When shooting, requires a special *variable speed motor.*

**Speaking Part**
Any actor who utters one single word of dialogue is considered to have a Speaking Part. They are underlined in red in the script and noted in the "Cast - Speaking" box on the breakdown sheets.

**Special Camera Operator**
To operate a "Panaglide" or "Steadicam" requires a specially trained camera operator.

**Special Effects**
Any effect which is special and must be created. See Chapter Four.

**Special Effects Department**
That division of the production crew, or sometimes a separate independent company, which is in charge of producing all the Special Effects on a production—from STAR WARS, to a practical sink.

**Special Portable Camera**
To shooting scenes which would not be possible with a standard camera, for example a chase scenes on foot, Panaglide and Steadicam (two brand names) are mounts which allow the camera to mount on the operator's body.

**Standard Script Format**
As illustrated in Chapter Three, there is a preferred way to type a motion picture screenplay. If other formats are used, it can affect your calculations in judging how much time it will take to shoot.

**Started**
Usually refers to the first day an actor works. As there are many rules governing an actor once he begins work, the proper start date is very important. See *drop-and-pick up, run of show, upgrade.*

**Strike**
To remove any equipment used in the shooting of a scene after the shooting has been completed. It is advisable not to strike a set until the *dailies* have been checked and approved.

**Stunt Coordinator**
The member of the crew responsible for the organization and coordination of the execution of all the stunts on a production.

**Stunt Doubles**
A stunt person who physically resembles a particular actor and performs any dangerous or potentially dangerous action for

that actor. For example, Mr. C is doubled in the burning Mercedes Benz sequence.

**Stunt Photo Double**
A stunt person who closely resembles (or is made to resemble) the actor and takes his place in dangerous or potentially dangerous scenes.

**Supporting Players**
The second leads in the film, e.g., Stanley, Paul, Martin, etc., are considered to be Supporting Players. They are underlined in red on the script and noted in the "Cast—Speaking" box on the breakdown sheets.

**Surveillance Equipment**
In THE CONVERSATION, the equipment which Harry Caul uses to track Ann and Mark is special, professional equipment which will have to be rented. Most likely, a *technical advisor* will also be hired.

**Teacher**
See *welfare worker.*

**Technical Advisor**
A person who is considered to be an expert in a certain field who can ensure the authenticity of a project. In THE CONVERSATION, the operation of the surveillance equipment would be overseen by a Technical Advisor.

**Transportation**
That department of the crew responsible for transporting the crew and all necessary equipment and vehicles for the production.

**Turn-Around Time**
The minimum and specific number of free time which must be given before that person may return to work without incurring

a penalty, e.g., an actor must be given 58 hours between completion Friday to start Monday morning

**Underline**
The recommended method for marking up a script. It is preferable to "highlighting," as the script is still legible when photocopied.

**Up-Grade**
To move to a higher pay classification. Usually used in reference to an actor. For example, an *extra* might be up-graded to a *silent bit* (or a *day player,* if given dialogue.)

**Variable Speed Motor**
A special motor which allows filming at rates other than 24 fps. See also *slow motion.*

**Vehicles**
Any car, truck, motorcycle, etc., which is used on the production. See also *picture cars, transportation.*

**Wardrobe**
Any item of clothing which is worn by the actors and mentioned in the screenplay. When doing a breakdown, it should be circled and noted in its appropriate column.

**Welfare Worker**
When a child under a certain age is hired, it is mandatory that a welfare worker teacher also be hired. See *child actors.*

**Wide Angle**
Camera's POV for shooting will be wider than normal, and may require the use of a wider angle lens.

**Wipe**
An Optical Effect used when the new scene literally "wipes" the previous scene from the screen. See *optical effect.*

**Wrapped**
To finish all required shooting: either at a location, for that day (night), or on the picture altogether.

**Zoom In**
When the camera appears to move toward the subject in a continuous take. This is usually done by using a *zoom lens.*

**Zoom Lens**
A special lens which allows the operator to move the image either closer or further away without moving the camera position.

**Zoom Out**
When the camera appears to move away from the subject in a continuous take. This is usually done by using a *zoom lens.*

# INDEX

*Note:* Entries after semicolon indicate glossary.

217

# ABOUT THE AUTHOR

Ralph S. Singleton works in the motion picture industry as a production manager/assistant director. He was head of production for Zoetrope Studios and was Production Manager on *Exposed* (MGM/UA), *One From The Heart* (Paramount), *The Winds of War* (USA–Paramount), *History of the World—Part I* (20th Century Fox), *Somebody Killed Her Husband* (Paramount), *Cagney & Lacey* (Orion), *Kojak* (Universal), etc.

He was also an Assistant Director on *Testament* (Paramount), *The Seduction of Joe Tynan* (20th Century Fox), *Greased Lightning* (Warner Bros.), *Taxi Driver* (Columbia), *Network* (Paramount), *The Front* (Warner Bros.), *Three Days of the Condor* (Paramount), *The Gambler* (Paramount), etc.

He is the only assistant director in the history of the Directors Guild of America to work on two Academy Award nominated films in the same year, and be nominated for the prestigious DGA award for both—*Network* and *Taxi Driver.* He is considered to be "one of the best production managers in the business." Mr. Singleton makes his home in Los Angeles, California.

**Francis Coppola's THE CONVERSATION**

KEY:
- Day Exterior
- Night Exterior
- Day Interior
- Night Interior
- Week Ending
- Holidays

**Production Board - Part II**

| D/N | Scene # | I/E | Location | Pages | Description |
|---|---|---|---|---|---|
| D | 230 | I | CATHOLIC CHURCH | 2/8 | GOES TO CONFESSION (1) |
| D | 231 | I | CONFESSIONAL | 4/8 | HE CONFESSES |
| D | 39 | I | NEIGHBORHOOD LAUNDRY | 5/8 | PICKS UP LAUNDRY; MAGIC (4) |
| N | 120 | I | HOTEL-AUDITORIUM | 3/8 | SLIDE SHOW + INSERTS ORLY |
| N | 123 | I | HOTEL-AUDITORIUM | 2/8 | C.U. BLUE BOX |
| N | 125 | I | HOTEL-AUDITORIUM | 1/8 | C.U. SLIDE "PRETTY WOMAN" |

**DAY 21**

*WEEK FOUR — HOLIDAY BREAK — CHRISTMAS & NEW YEARS*

| D/N | Scene # | I/E | Location | Pages | Description |
|---|---|---|---|---|---|
| D | 232-236 | E | CONTINENTAL LODGE | 5/8 | WATCHES; ENTERS LODGE (15) |
| D | 237 | I | CONT. LODGE-LOBBY | 3/8 | HE REGISTERS (10) 36 |
| D | 238 | I | CONT. LODGE-CORRIDOR | 2/8 | WALKS TO DOOR (2) |
| N | 254 | I | CONT. LODGE-CORRIDOR | 1/8 | WALKS TO ROOM B-7 |

**DAY 22**

| D/N | Scene # | I/E | Location | Pages | Description |
|---|---|---|---|---|---|
| D | 239-240 | I | MOTEL-BEDROOM | 2/8 | WALKS THROUGH ROOM |
| D | 241 | I | MOTEL-BATHROOM | 1 1/8 | EAVESDROPPING-MOVES AWAY |
| D | 245-250 | I | MOTEL-BEDROOM | 1 | HEARS FIGHT - HIDES |
| N | 251-253 | I | MOTEL-BEDROOM | 3/8 | WAKES UP, LEAVES |

**DAY 23**

| D/N | Scene # | I/E | Location | Pages | Description |
|---|---|---|---|---|---|
| N | 255-260 | I | B-7 MOTEL BEDROOM | 6/8 | CHECKS OUT ROOM |
| N | 261-268 | I | B-7 MOTEL BATHROOM | 1 1/8 | DISCOVERS BLOOD |
| N | 270 | E | CONTINENTAL LODGE | 1/8 | WALKS AWAY, UPSET (25) |
| N | 359 | I | B-7 MOTEL-BATHROOM | 1/8 | C.U. BLOODY FOOTPRINTS |
| N | 269 | I | B-7 MOTEL BEDROOM | 4/8 | OPENS WINDOW |

**DAY 24**

*WEEK FIVE*

| D/N | Scene # | I/E | Location | Pages | Description |
|---|---|---|---|---|---|
| D | 363 | I | B-7 MOTEL-BEDROOM | 2/8 | MR. C. PLAYS TAPE |
| D | 359/361 | I | B-7 MOTEL | 5/8 | KILL MR.C. (M) |
| D | 356 | I | B-7 MOTEL-BATHROOM | 3/8 | CLEAN UP BLOOD |

**DAY 25**

| D/N | Scene # | I/E | Location | Pages | Description |
|---|---|---|---|---|---|
| D | 289 | E | BUS NO. 1 | 1/8 | BUS IN FOG — 37 |
| D | 285 | E/ | BUS NO. 1 | 1/8 | ANN SITS ALONE — 37 |
| D | 289 | E | BUS NO. 1 | 1/8 | BUS MOVES UP HILL — 37 |
| D | 291 | E | BUS NO. 1 | 1/8 | BUS TURNS TO RIGHT — 37 |
| D/N | 298 | E | BUS NO. 1 | 3/8 | HARRY GETS ON W/ANN — 37 |
| LATE DAY | 300-302 | I | BUS NO. 1 | 1 | HARRY TALKS TO ANN — 37 |
| LATE DAY | 299 | E | BUS NO. 1 | 1/8 | ANN IGNORES HARRY — 37 |
| N | 305-304 | E | BUS NO. 1 | 2/8 | HARRY REPEATS TAPE — 37 |
| N | 305-306 | E | BUS NO. 1 | 6/8 | ANN RUNS, HARRY FOLLOWS — 37 |
| N | 307-308 | I | BUS NO. 1 | 3/8 | MOVING VIEW OF HARRY — 38 |
| N | 287 | E | BUS NO. 2 + STREET | 1/8 | H'S POV - BUS NO.1 (REAR) — 38 |
| N | 288 | E | BUS NO. 2 + STREET | 1/8 | BUS #2 CLIMBS HILL — 38 |
| N | 292 | E | BUS NO. 2 + STREET | 1/8 | HARRY WATCHES ANN'S BUS — 38 |
| N | 293 | E | BUS NO. 2 + STREET | 1/8 | BUS #2 DOESN'T TURN RIGHT — 38 |
| N | 295 | E | BUS NO. 2 + STREET | 1/8 | BUS #2 TURN RIGHT — 38 |
| N | 296 | E | BUS NO. 2 + STREET | 3/8 | HARRY GETS UP + OFF BUS — 38 |
| D | 286 | I | POLES + LINES (INSERTS) | 1/8 | WIRES SHORT |
| D | 290 | I | POLES + LINES | 1/8 | WIRES SEPARATE |
| D | 294 | I | POLES + LINES (INSERTS) | 2/8 | ANTENNAE GLIDE STRAIGHT |
| D | 297 | I | BUS NO. 1 + STREET | 1/8 | HARRY FALLS GETTING OFF BUS — 38 |

**DAY 26**

| D/N | Scene # | I/E | Location | Pages | Description |
|---|---|---|---|---|---|
| N | 309/316 | E | STREET-STEEP | 1 | CHASE ON FOOT |
| N | 317/332 | E | THE PARK | 3 5/8 | CHASES, TALKS TO ANN |

**DAY 27**

| D/N | Scene # | I/E | Location | Pages | Description |
|---|---|---|---|---|---|
| D | 380/397 | E | HARRY'S APARTMENT | 2 7/8 | SEARCHES FOR WIRETAP |

**DAY 28**

*THE END*